FELL AND HILL RUNNING

by Norman Matthews and Dennis Quinlan

Cover photograph
Mark Rigby, Scottish Champion 1995, leaving Pike of Blisco summit in the Langdale Horseshoe.

First Edition 1996

ISBN 0 85134 138 1 1.5K/06.96

225A Bristol Road
Birmingham B5 7UB

Typeset in Times, designed and printed on 115gsm Fineblade Cartridge in England by Woodcote Limited, Epsom, Surrey KT18 7HL.

Foreword

It has been said that a willing volunteer is worth more than 10 pressed men. In this case two volunteers took on the task of writing *Fell and Hill Running*, not because we were the leading authorities but because we were willing and available. We hope that this introduction will enhance your enjoyment of running the fells and help to introduce those runners who have yet to experience the pleasure.

The Authors

Photographs by Peter Hartley

Peter Hartley came to fell running from a background of climbing and mountaineering in 1972. His initial interest was in two day mountain marathons and other long navigational type events, but as training and fitness increased he ran races of all distances as a member of Rossendale Harriers. Being a keen photographer, he wanted to try to capture some of the atmosphere of the sport and various sights and conditions a fell runner experiences when racing in all weathers at all times of the year, and he has taken many photographs whilst competing in races. A car accident interrupted and then eventually ended his competitive running career following a hip replacement in 1993. He still attends many fell races, but now as a photographer, and contributes regularly to the *Fell Runner, Athletics Weekly* and other magazines covering the sport.

Additional photographs have been supplied by John Hardman (page 1, courtesy Westmorland Gazette), Roger Ingham (page 2), Bob Douglas (page 43, right) and Norman Matthews (pages 53 and 55).

About the Authors

Norman Matthews

Norman Matthews started his fell running career aged 38 in 1976, after fifteen years as a Martial Arts instructor. His running achievements have thus been confined to the veteran's categories which culminated in his British and English Championship wins in 1990, although a brief excursion on the Cross Country scene in 1989 and 1991 gained him County titles. His retirement from the Automobile Association in 1992 allowed him to coach full time and to pursue his ambition to introduce a coaching structure into Fell Running. He has coached athletes from Junior to Senior Internationals, both on Fell and Road, and to World Champion in the veteran's ranks. A BAF Senior Coach in both Endurance and Fell Running, Norman's ambition is to see Fell Running receive the same International recognition by the IAAF as other athletic disciplines.

Dennis Quinlan

Dennis Quinlan has been involved in athletics since the age of fourteen and was an English Schools Cross-Country Champion. As a senior athlete he represented the Republic of Ireland at Cross Country, Road and Track. As a Super-Vet he represented England at Cross-Country and was British 5k Road Champion. In his day he was a leading veteran fell runner. He began advising others as an undergraduate at Leeds University in the early sixties and has continued to do so throughout his athletic career. He has guided runners from outright beginners to those attaining the highest standards, including several Internationals on Fell, Track, Road and Cross-Country. He has advised the England World Trophy Mountain Team and is a BAF Senior Coach/Fell. He has written many articles about distance running, including those for the short-lived but popular *'Up & Down'* magazine in the early nineties.

Contents

Acknowledgements

To all those who helped in providing material for this booklet, especially Bill Smith, Danny Hughes, and Steve Pearson, and to Carl Johnson whose enthusiasm for introducing a coaching syllabus for Fell Running was appreciated and highly motivating.

CHAPTER 1

Introduction and History

The Lake District is generally regarded as being the birthplace of fell racing, but the earliest event known to us actually took place in Scotland. In 1064, King Malcolm Canmore organised a race up Creag Choinnich above Braemar in order to choose a suitable runner to carry dispatches over rough country. There were prizes on offer to the winner, who turned out to be the youngest of three McGregor brothers from nearby Ballochbuie. This event is now considered to be the precursor of Highland Games in general and the Braemar Gathering in particular, the hill race of the latter using the same course up to 1850.

Guide Races

Hill racing is a feature of numerous Highland Games, some of which boast formidable histories, and many of the ancient village sports and country fairs of Northern England, some of which date back to the Middle Ages and earlier, no doubt also included a fell race, though unfortunately it wasn't until around 1850 that records of such events began to be kept.

Bill Teasdale

The first known Grasmere Guides race, originally held as an event for professional mountain guides to test their speed and agility against each other, took place in 1868. The Burnsall Fell Race in Wharfedale was certainly being run prior to 1880. Another Yorkshire race at Lothersdale, south of Skipton, was being contested at least as early as 1847, and such notable events as Kilnsey Crag and Coniston Gullies also date back to the 19th century.

These races were all short up-and-down courses with strong spectator appeal and were "professional" in that money prizes were to be won. However, the 1878 and '79 Grasmere races were contested by both professionals and amateurs, including the famous Choppy Warburton from Rossendale who was defeated by John Greenop of Langdale, a Grasmere winner on six consecutive occasions, 1876-81.

Ernest Dalzell being congratulated by Lord Lonsdale after one of his Grasmere victories. On the right is Dalzell's trainer, Jack Cowperthwaite of Keswick.

The formation of the Amateur Athletic Association in 1880 resulted in most of the early fell races of the South Pennines being amateur events. They were located close to the industrial areas and therefore to the growing ranks of amateur athletic clubs. These included the Hallam Chase near Sheffield (inaugurated in 1863 but under AAA Laws since 1925), Rivington Pike in Lancashire (1893) and Eccles Pike in Derbyshire (1910).

The name of Ernest Dalzell, a Keswick gamekeeper whose distinguished fell racing career was terminated by an enemy bullet in France during the First World War, is one of the most revered in the history of the sport. But the Caldbeck shepherd, Bill Teasdale, MBE, who dominated the sport during the 1950s and 60s, is regarded by enthusiasts as the greatest short-course fell runner ever. His "King of the Fells" crown was inherited by Fred Reeves of Coniston, a powerful climber who was undoubtedly the most successful professional runner of the 1970s, though overshadowed as a steep, rough descender by his great rival, Tommy Sedgwick, who triumphed on twelve occasions over the intimidating Alva Highland Games course which carries the British Hill Racing Championship title.

Early Amateur Races

Athletes who contested early amateur races

did not consider themselves to be strictly fell runners and would have been more at home on road, track or cross-country. The most adept of them was T.P. "Pat" Campbell of Salford Harriers, an international steeplechaser and cross-country runner, whose fell triumphs during the late 1920s and 1930s included nine wins at Rivington Pike, and three each at Eccles Pike and Burnsall.

The Rivington Race from Horwich had been run from 1893 to 1900 and revived under the AAA Laws in 1929 while the Burnsall event changed its status from professional to amateur in 1932, a move followed by several other events in later years. The fell race at Harden Moss Sheepdog Trials was introduced in 1937 and is the only one of a number of like events in the Huddersfield area which has survived on a regular basis, not counting the long Marsden-Edale Trog which was revived in 1973. Two well known Yorkshire athletes who enjoyed success at both Harden Moss and Burnsall during the 1950s and '60s were Pete Watson (Bramley) who achieved eight victories at Harden Moss and seven at Burnsall, and Dave Hodgson (Leeds St. Marks) who was double winner at both events.

In Scotland, the Ben Nevis Race from Fort William was revived in 1937 following events in 1899 and 1903, around which period several solo "time trials" had also taken place, including four by women. There was another lapse from 1944 to 1951, since when it has been organised each year by the Ben Nevis Race Association. Prominent during the 1950's were local athletes Brian Kearney and Eddie Campbell (Lochaber) who accomplished three victories each. The 1955 race heralded the "English invasion" of the Ben race with three entrants from south of the border, including Joe Hand from Carlisle who finished second.

Long Distance

Joe Hand had already distinguished himself in England by winning the third Lake District Mountain Trial the previous year and he completed a consecutive hat-trick of victories in 1956. The first five events, including three from Langdale, were run over a previously disclosed course, with the mountain navigation event which prevails today being introduced in 1957. The most successful Mountain Trialists have been Jos Naylor MBE (Cumberland FR) with ten wins 1967-79, and Billy Bland (Borrowdale FR) with nine, 1978-91.

April, 1954 saw the first Three Peaks Race in Yorkshire being won by its organiser, Fred Bagley (Preston H.), the course following a traditional walkers' route over the Craven summits of Ingleborough, Penyghent and Whernside, with considerable road and cross-country running in between. For this reason, it began to attract entries from ordinary club runners anxious to prove themselves over what is certainly a very hard course, though few of those athletes have ventured to try the much more demanding Mountain Trial or other long Lakeland events like the Ennerdale Horseshoe and Wasdale, which are routed over rough mountain terrain. 1968 saw the introduction of the Two-Day Two-Man Mountain Marathon, later to become known as the "Karrimor". This is a mountain navigation event demanding orienteering skills and is held in a different part of Britain each year. Its success has inspired similar two day mountain races in other parts of the UK.

Interest in long distance fell running of another kind had already been revived in 1960 when Alan Heaton and Stan Bradshaw of Clayton-le-Moors Harriers became the first men to complete "Bob Graham's Round of the Fells" in the Lake District within 24 hours since Graham's own achievement in 1932, which had been a development from earlier 24 hour circuits dating back to 1864. Graham's route had covered 42 peaks. In 1965 Heaton set a new 24 hour record of 60 peaks, which Jos Naylor raised to 72 peaks in 1975 and Mark McDermott (Kendal) to 76 peaks in 1988. The Bob Graham Round has now become a standard test course for long distance fell runners and has inspired numerous other long distance mountain records in various parts of Britain.

The F.R.A.

1971 witnessed the formation of the Fell Runners Association which has since gone from strength to strength as the sport's major governing body for amateur races. In 1972 it promoted the first annual championship, using a system devised by Mike Davies (Reading), an outstanding fell runner of the 1960s. Davies was also responsible for the method of classifying events into three categories of severity: A, B and C. Various ways of awarding championship points have since been tried. In 1996 the British Championship involves one short, two medium and one long A category races. Outstanding champions have included ex-professional Kenny Stuart (Keswick) and Colin Donnelly (Eryri) with three wins each, Mike Short (Horwich) John Wild (Cumberland FR) and Mark Kinch (Warrington AC) with two each.

Ladies' fell racing under AAA Laws began in 1977, though there had been occasional female competitors in long mountain races prior to this. The first ladies' championship was held in 1979 and the most prominent athletes have been Angela Brand-Barker (Eryri) with four victories, two achieved under her maiden name of Carson, and Pauline Howarth (Keswick) with three. The outstanding female in the realm of ultra-distance mountain running has been Helen Diamantides (Ambleside).

International Events

The seeds of international fell racing were sown during the 1970s with a few Scandinavian and Swiss orienteers producing superlative performances in the Karrimor and some English runners competing in the Sierre-Zinal race in Switzerland and Pikes Peak Marathon in the USA. However, most Continental races are routed over "fast" runnable terrain, with uphill-only courses being strongly favoured.

When the annual World Trophy event was inaugurated by the Italians in 1985, therefore, this type of course was chosen with the result that the British specialists, accustomed to rougher terrain, generally found they were no match for the Continentals, particularly the Italians who have easily been the most successful nation so far. However, Britain has not been entirely lacking in World Trophy race winners: Kenny Stuart won in 1985 and Martin Jones (Horwich) in both 1992 and 1993, whilst among the ladies the accomplished all-rounder Carol Greenwood (Bingley) emerged victorious in 1986 as did Beverley Redfern (Carnethy) in 1990.

Fell racing has now established itself as a worthy sport in its own right, with over 350 races in the 1996 fixtures calendar as compared with 42 in 1971, and its future certainly looks bright.

World Cup Juniors
Bedwyn Hughes (Wales), Keswick 1988.

Billy McKay (Northern Ireland) on Grisedale Pike.

Rod Philbeam leading the England Team through Keswick to the Opening Ceremony, World Cup 1988.

The Scottish Team during the World Cup Mountain Races at Keswick in 1988.

Race Courses

All races within the FRA calendar clearly indicate the race category and also state junior races when offered at the event. The age categories for the junior races are specified within the race details. The record for the course distance is also shown for men and women, which gives some indication of race duration.
The races are run to laid down safety standards applied by the FRA and upheld by the race organisers.

SHORT RACES
Many of the short races are also part of a village fair or gala weekend, and make an ideal family outing. These races are a good way to start fell running, with little in the way of navigation required, and events are usually under 30 minutes in duration.

MEDIUM RACES
These are suitable for those runners who have already competed in the shorter races, and also for those with a running background who are looking for more of a challenge. Some of the medium races do require a knowledge of map reading, especially if weather conditions are inclement at the time.

LONG RACES
Only those runners with a good knowledge of fell running and medium race experience should attempt the long "A" races. There are occasions on fine sunny days when, with a long procession of runners to follow, complacency may allow a runner to under-estimate the potential dangers of running for long periods of time on mountainous terrain.

Map reading skills are an integral part of fell running and play an important part in guiding a runner to safety when adverse conditions are prevalent. These navigational skills are a prerequisite for the medium and long races, and at times helpful in the short races. Weather conditions can play a major part in determining the race duration. Unlike road Marathons, the long "A" races have no facility for organised food or drink stations and runners must supply their own, usually carrying them in a bumbag.

3 Peaks Race 1991.
Sarah Rowell approaching the summit of Ingleborough on her way to a new record (one of many).

CHAPTER 2

Safety and Navigation

Safety should be the first consideration that the coach makes when planning the many aspects of training in Fell Running.

CONCEPT OF SAFETY

Preventative measures are the hallmark of a good safety policy. The fell side in adverse weather conditions is not the place to learn hard lessons. Good planning and adherence to safety guidelines will allow fell runners to enjoy the sport without putting their lives or the lives of others at risk. Runners to their cost find out at times of accident or injury how lonely the fells can become. Fell running by its nature has more natural hazards than any other running sport. The coach must be aware that an athlete who has no fell running experience could possibly put safety at risk if attempting a long 'A' race in bad weather conditions without the necessary training and equipment to meet such demands. The mistake of comparing a road marathon with a similar distance over the fells can become more than an unpleasant experience; the potential consequences of bad pace judgment in the latter are a good deal more serious than in the former.

Without taking away the spirit of fell running, with all the thrills and occasional spills, it is necessary to make all athletes aware of the dangers in fell running and to ensure that all unnecessary risks are avoided.

NAVIGATION

This section should be read with map and compass to hand.

Unfortunately, the art of map reading is not considered a prerequisite by the majority of fell runners and a field is usually divided into those that lead and those that follow, with the latter usually in the majority. Unlike orienteering that has staggered starts with the obvious necessity for competence in map reading, a fell race with its mass start can lead to a degree of complacency, with runners having limited map reading skills.

Pete Bland leading a group heading out of the Langdale Valley in the Blisco Dash.

In clear weather navigation is mostly a matter of interpreting the map in the light of what can be seen around you. Expertise at this can only come with practice. Also, in good weather, with a significant number of runners in a race, following the tail or string of runners can usually provide for an incident free run. But when weather conditions are inclement, with limited visibility, problems can and usually do occur with route finding. There is the added risk in the competitive atmosphere of racing of suspending normal precautions. The philosophy of 'follow my leader' can be a dangerous practice and basic skills in map reading need to be taught. The following represents a minimum introduction and both coach and athlete are advised to read further. The basic principles of a compass must be known with the differences of Grid North and Magnetic North clearly understood.

Magnetic North

The north to which the compass needle always points, and which changes half a degree every 3 years. Currently, in 1996, magnetic north is estimated at about 5 deg. west of grid north. Up to date information can be found on the inside of the Ordnance Survey map and this is essential knowledge for coach and athlete.

Grid North

The north pointed to by the grid lines on the map, 5 deg. east of magnetic north.

The National Grid Reference

All Ordnance Survey maps with at least a scale of 2cm to 1km (1.25in to 1 mile) show the national grid. The instructions on how to take a map reference, using a particular example from the map in question, are clearly explained on the map and should be learned.

Type of map

Various scales of map are available; the 1:25 000 (2.5″ to 1 mile) is the most popular map for fell runners showing the fell side in great detail, although the 1:50 000 (1.25″ to 1 mile) series can in most cases be sufficient. Water-resistant maps for many areas can be bought, but it is simple to cut out routes and cover the map with thin, transparent, self-adhesive covering for yourself. The skill of interpreting the map and understanding the lie of the land comes with practice. Navigation in clear weather is largely based on relating the map to the terrain and rarely requires the use of a compass. However, because of weather uncertainty the proper use of a compass is essential.

Compass Techniques

A. How to Stay on Course

Let us suppose you are on a fell following an indistinct path. You know your position on the map and your destination is a mountain peak you can see some miles ahead of you (Figure 1). You notice some low cloud coming down which will obscure your destination. Take your compass and point the direction-of-travel arrow at the peak you wish to reach. Turn the compass housing until the arrow on the base of the housing points in the same direction as the north (red) end of the compass needle. Keep the compass needle and the arrow on the base of the housing in line and follow the direction-of-travel arrow. Rather than keeping the eye glued to the direction-of-travel arrow, it is easier and more accurate to find an object such as a cairn, tree or boulder on the line of the path somewhere near the limit of the visibility and run towards it repeating the process until the destination is reached.

Fig. 1 How to stay on course

B. Plotting a Course from the Map (Figure 2)

Very often paths link well-defined features. A path rarely curves across a field and even in mountainous country they are often fairly straight unless following a natural feature such as a stream. Using an Ordnance Survey map and compass, it is possible to plot your course beforehand by noting down the compass bearing at each point the path changes direction.

The method is as follows: (1) Place the map on a flat surface. It is not necessary to orientate it (i.e. position it so that the northern edge faces north).

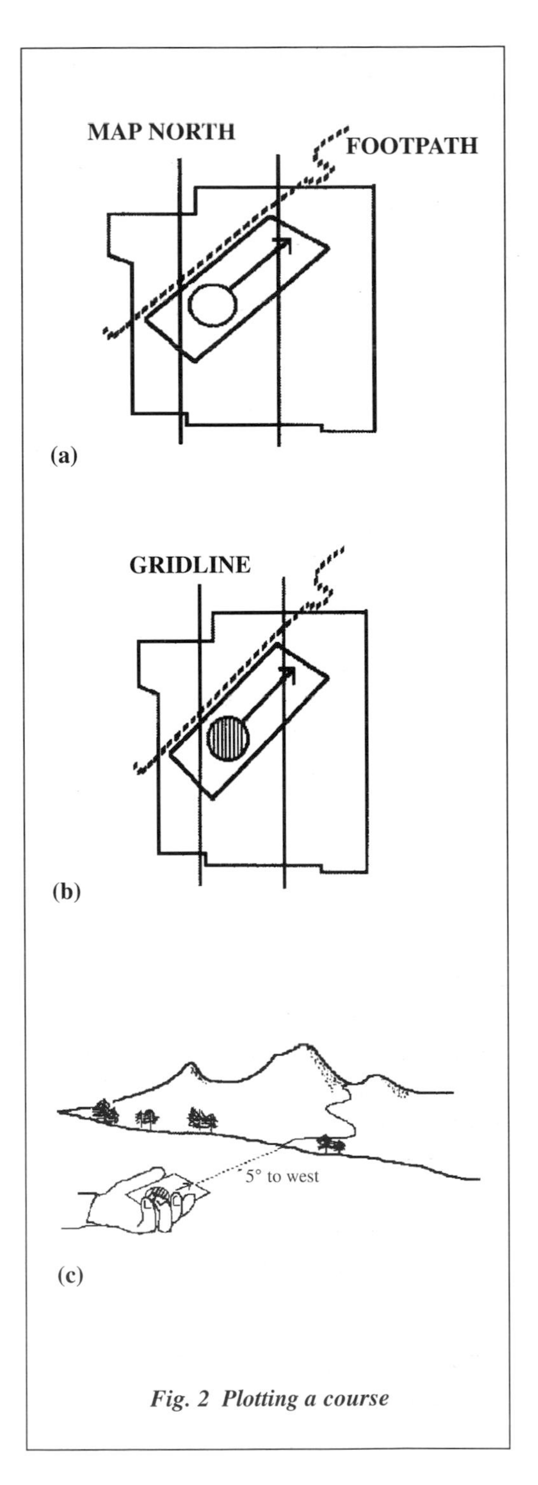

Fig. 2 Plotting a course

(2) Place the straight perspex base of the compass along the line of the path to be followed (Figure 2a).

(3) Without moving the base, turn the compass housing until the arrow in the compass housing points towards the north end of the map and is exactly parallel to the north-south grid lines (Figure 2b).

(4) In order to get the arrow in the compass housing to point to grid north it is necessary to **ADD** the magnetic variation found at the bottom of the map by moving the compass housing the appropriate number of degrees.

(5) Read off the bearing from the point indicated on compass and note it down. When reaching that point in the race set the compass for that bearing and, holding it in your hand, turn your body until the red arrow in the compass housing is in line with the north-pointing needle.

(6) The line of the path runs where the direction-of-travel arrow on the base plate of the compass is pointing (see Figure 2c).

C. Finding Your Exact Position on the Map

Very often you may be running along a path and, although you are not lost, you wish to know your precise position on that path. Your position can be found as follows:

(1) Select a prominent landmark which can be identified both on the ground and on the map.

(2) Point the direction-of-travel arrow at the landmark.

(3) Turn the compass housing so that the arrow on the base lines up with the north-facing needle.

(4) **Subtract** the difference between magnetic north and grid north by moving the compass housing the correct amount.

(5) Place the base plate of the compass on the map with the long edge touching the landmark from which the bearing has been taken.

(6) Without altering the position of the compass housing, turn the base plate on the map until the arrow on the base of the compass housing is exactly parallel to the grid lines.

(7) Where the edge of the base plate intersects the line of the footpath is your exact position. This process is known as taking a back bearing.

D. Finding Your Position When Completely Lost

Being 'lost' usually means that you know to within a mile or two, hopefully less, your position but need to identify exactly where you are. Examine the map and note carefully the last time you were absolutely certain of your position. This can usually be done by some physical feature such as a stream, or hill, but do make certain that you crossed the stream at the right point and that it was the right hill. Assuming that you can mark on the map your last known position, mark off the direction in which you travelled, if necessary by taking a bearing with your compass. Next, estimate the time taken and /or the distance covered since your last known position and mark this estimated position on the map. You should now have a fairly clear idea of where you are. Orientate the map by setting the compass at 360 deg. and placing the base plate on the north-south grid lines. Next turn the map and compass without disturbing the position of the compass until the north facing arrow points to 355 deg. The map is then set exactly and it should be possible to recognise certain features such as hills (from the shape of their contours).

Select two features and take a bearing from each of them as described in paragraph C above. Where the two lines intersect is your approximate position. Ideally, you should take three back bearings which should produce a small triangle within which you stand, giving a more accurate location of your position. You will then be able to take another compass bearing to rejoin the path at some appropriate point. If it proves impossible to locate your position, there is nothing to be done but to retrace your steps until you reach a point which you can definitely identify.

An introduction into basic navigational skills should be taught from the outset, even though most runners graduate from short races where map reading is usually not necessary. It is essential that fell coaches ensure that runners who participate in fell running have a rudimentary knowledge of basic map reading, and have the ability to use a compass as outlined.

As the runner progresses to 'A' class medium and eventually 'A' class long, it is also essential to have wider skills in map reading. Course reconnoitering and good map reading play an important part in race preparation, and this aspect of coaching can play a critical role in the overall performance and safety of an athlete in race conditions.

The FRA has for some time taken the initiative in preparing runners in mountain navigation, with regular weekend courses. Those interested should contact the FRA secretary, c/o British Athletic Federation, 225a Bristol Road, Birmingham B5 7UB.

The FRA Handbook contains an extensive list of 'Safety Requirements for Fell Races' and other information including specific details of all races, their grading, facilities and course records. It is required reading, so membership is strongly advised.

The same publication contains up-to-date details of officials and necessary contact numbers.

It is good safety practice to ensure that someone is aware of your intended route on the fells when out running and knows the estimated time of return.

Descending Ingleborough in the 3 Peaks Race, heading for Sulber Nick and the finish at Horton.

Wilf Brindle at Winter Hill following a well established route.

Chapter 3

Equipment and Weather

Race Preparation

Preparation starts with knowledge of the route. There is no substitute for reconnoitering the race route beforehand if this is feasible for the athlete, and acceptable to the race organiser and land owner.

If it has not been possible to check the race route, then every effort should be made to study the route on the map, and confer with knowledgeable friends as to the various route choices. The race route should be sketched on the map and various compass readings taken and recorded for easy reference, either on the map or sellotaped to the compass. Attention should be given to all those features that in clear weather will assist in staying on course, with obvious thought given to the fact that on the day any such references may not be visible. The location of streams should be noted for drinking stations.

Clothing & Footwear

Choice of what to wear in a particular race on a given day can vary from runner to runner. The judgement of impending weather conditions at varying heights in the race, and the most suitable clothing for such conditions, can play a major role in the athlete's performance and safety.

The British weather is unpredictable at most times of the year and it is worth remembering that conditions on the tops of mountains are often far more severe than at the start, especially with the wind chill effect, and that in fell running a misjudgement of the weather can occasionally be life threatening. Compulsory clothing items and equipment are now the norm on long or arduous courses. Race organisers can insist, under Rule 9 of the FRA safety requirements, what clothing and equipment will be worn or carried. A range of clothing for selection should thus be taken to the race and be available on the day.

Derek Brown (Clayton) coming to grief on the greasy rocks of the river crossing at Buckden Pike.

Full Waterproof Cover
It is a good habit to keep full rainsuit body cover, hat, gloves, whistle and compass permanently in a bumbag for all events - then don't forget the map of the course! Rip stop nylon has for some time been favoured because it is light and compact, fitting readily inside the bumbag. There are now various products on the market that allow a range of choice, from lightweight shower proof material to fully waterproof Gortex. The runner must balance warmth against the prevailing conditions and the constraints of weight. That choice can only be made if many options are available at the race venue, and so a variety of equipment is best taken. The waterproof over-trousers must have the facility to be easily fitted over fell shoes. Waterproof garments offer no friction resistance if a runner loses footing on steep inclines in snowy conditions - a rapid descent follows!

Thermal Gear
Thermal top and bottoms are an essential part of fell running kit. A variety of bottom lengths are useful, from thigh warmers to knee cover and full leg cover. It is not often that FULL gear needs to be worn, but once again the option must be available at race start.

Gloves
These can range from thin thermal wear to waterproof mittens, all depending on weather conditions and a runner's circulation efficiency. It is important to stress the need to keep the hands warm, not just for the sake of comfort, but because a runner's ability to read a map and work a compass rely on hands that work!

Tony Hesketh (Horwich RMI) well wrapped up against the weather during the Haworth Hobble.

Head Wear
Bob hats come in all shapes and sizes. Make sure yours is sufficiently close fitting to stay on in strong wind and can cover the ears if necessary. Those experienced in winter fell running use a balaclava that is folded into a hat, and is adaptable for all eventualities.

Running Socks
It is always an advantage to have several pairs of socks available. Usually a clothing item that receives little attention, socks can prove a major distraction if not fitted correctly. Inadequate socks that fold or slip inside the shoes can result in blistering.

Shoes
Shoes are undoubtedly the most important

item of equipment in maintaining personal safety on the fells. Although waterproofs and winter gear are essential on certain days, a suitable pair of fell shoes are necessary at most races. Specialised fell shoes have deep set moulded studs and the midsole cushioning is kept to a minimum, creating a low profile and enabling more stability on uneven terrain. These shoes can now be purchased widely from sports shoes stockists or from specialised fell running shops. The shoes are lightweight and robust, with specially reinforced areas to protect the shoe from rock edges. In dry conditions certain fell races with well defined tracks can accommodate a suitable pair of lightweight road shoes. A wider range of studded shoes are available from Scandinavian countries through orienteering retail outlets.

For those who specialise in short steep races with all grass terrain a fully spiked fell shoe with heel spikes can be a distinct advantage.

More injuries are caused in fell running from falling when descending than any other type of injury.

A new pair of fell shoes will not guarantee that falls do not occur, but a sound pair of studded shoes will go a long way in ensuring a runner stays upright longer. In the younger age groups it is essential that their shoes match the terrain when learning the art of descending.

Shoes should keep the foot firm and in line; this is particularly important for athletes with an over-pronation or other malalignment problem. The uneven terrain, contouring and wet shoes can all add to the problem of instability. If this area is neglected injuries will surely result. Other measures worth considering are taping or orthotics. Taping correctly requires either the initial services of a physiotherapist or coach, as the tape pressure needs to resist the movement of the foot in the direction of supination or

The essential studded sole unit of fell shoes.

pronation, depending upon individual foot movement.

The fitting of orthotics requires professional advice, especially for fell runners. Athletes with significantly different sizes between left and right feet should consider a special order from an established manufacturer in fell shoes.

Bumbags

Wearing a bumbag only when racing is poor preparation. The habit must be formed in training. It should fit close to the body, affording no movement when running. To obtain this, it is necessary to have small intermediate straps on the bag as well as the main fastener. Experiment with a full load of what you may expect to carry. The bag should be waterproof and enable easy access.

Whistle & Compass

Always remember when in difficulty and when help is required, that six distinct blasts on the whistle is the distress signal, followed by a minute's pause. This is continued until help has arrived. Carrying a compass is compulsory in some races, so knowledge of using it would seem to be essential too! For those who normally wear glasses, selection of a compass with a large magnifying section is essential for those times when rainy conditions make wearing glasses impossible.

Survival Bag

This is an essential item of equipment for full day or longer events. If you are caught out in the cold with an injury that prohibits walking, get into the bag as quickly as possible. Try to find a suitable place to lie down without rocks or sharp edges, with as much insulation underneath as possible, and blow your whistle. The golden rule, if you can walk, is to lose height safely in the direction of the race route, towards a check point or road crossing. Think before you make your decision and play safe, making for the nearest route contact point, preferably not climbing and certainly not climbing into worse weather. Put on your

A clutch of balaclavas anticipating the worst from the "Beast", Wadsworth Trog.

Bumbags being used to carry full body protection.

full waterproof cover, gloves and any other clothing you have with you and eat if any food is available. Do not forget to inform race control of your retirement as soon as possible.

Rucksacks

In mountain marathons, choice of a suitable rucksack is essential. Again there is no substitute for trying the sack out in training, not only for the effect of running with the weight, but more so for the comfort and fit. The shoulder straps need to be lightly padded and wide with the chest straps comfortable to wear. Adjustment to keep the sack well positioned on the back and not sagging down is essential. Today's modern versions have a range of netting and outside pockets that allow you easy access for essentials during the run.

Summer Conditions

Not all hazardous conditions are created by cold weather. Although most precautions are taken during the winter months there are times when the sun can equally cause problems.

Dehydration

Dehydration is common on the fells in summer. What some runners consider to be the effects of the race distance, or lack of training, may well be a loss of fluid. It is important to hydrate well before any race, especially those in sunny conditions and those in the medium and long categories. Drink plenty of water in the 24 hours prior to the event, and before the race start. Unlike road races, fell running organisers usually provide little or no food or drink during the race. As drinks are necessary during the race, mountain streams should be noted on the map before the event. If little water is available en route then a water bottle will have to be carried.

Sun's Rays

The simple precaution of using sun block cream is often overlooked. Exposure to the sun for hours at a time can be a serious problem, especially at altitude. Watch out for too liberal an application around the eyes where sweating can cause irritation. Hands and thighs should also be kept clear. A sweatband on the forehead or on the wrist can be helpful. A suitable cap with a large peak can also prove invaluable. In extreme temperatures wearing a dampened neckerchief around the neck or attached to the back of the cap is beneficial.

Blisters

On a warm day in races with long hard path descents like Snowdon and Skiddaw, blisters usually occur for those who descend at pace. Taping and plasters are recommended. Vaseline can also be effective, but good fitting shoes and socks go a long way in reducing the worst effects.

> All your clothing should be tested in training before being used in races. To find out during a race that your Lycra bottoms are continually falling down when wet, or your waterproof trousers will not pull over your fell shoes, is very distracting, and can affect your concentration and decision-making.

Roger Bell (Ambleside) dwarfed by the magnificent landscape at the Langdale Horseshoe.

CHAPTER 4

Training for the Fells

Training for the fells is like training for any other distance events in that best performances depend mainly on a consistent volume of training. For many fell runners the bulk of this training can be done, and is, on undulating off-road surfaces or road. Even fell runners who live in mountainous localities are unlikely to train daily on severe climbs. They are fortunate, of course, in having them available for some of their training.

However, there are one or two significant differences between fell and other events. The most obvious are the demands of steep climbing and steep descending, both of which require practice. That practice for many lies almost entirely in racing, but better results are gained from incorporating both in training. Less obvious differences are the range of events commonly undertaken and the frequency of racing. Races can vary from the little over a mile of Burnsall to the arduous 23 miles of Ennerdale - and for many the 2 day mountain marathon. What is unusual about the fells is the number of competitors who participate across the full range of events. The Championship structure, of course, encourages that range of participation, demanding as it does competition from 'A' Short to 'A' Long.

Climbing training

The strength to climb will automatically be developed through 'hilly runs', especially if a degree of extra concentration is applied to the climbs. This, along with races, is what many do. However, it is particularly beneficial to incorporate at least one repetition hill session into the weekly training programme.

Endurance hill reps

The total climbing time for these would probably be in the range of 15-25 min and the climbs might take 2-3 min each. A brisk descent is desirable to keep the recovery tight and so **maximising the endurance benefit**. The climbing is meant to be hard but a little short of race intensity. It is likely that race intensity would be touched towards the end of the climb, but it is important to the purpose of this session that it is not maintained. For those with the benefit of a heart rate monitor the pulse range largely aimed for would be between 5-10 beats less than the typical pulse experienced in a half hour race. An adequate warm up and cool down, followed by stretching, should accompany the session. Flexibility and mobility exercises are important ingredients in the training of athletes who would look to run fast as their neglect limits the power and range of movement in fast, explosive running in particular.

Provided the recovery is kept tight, ie no more and preferably less than the time taken to do the climb, there is nothing magical in the **length of the climb.** The key factors are the total size of the session and the controlled intensity.

The **severity** of the climb is important in judging this session right. It is very difficult to run up a severe climb and keep the effort within the above parameters because running at almost any pace up a very steep climb is very demanding. The way to handle this is for the athlete to walk a little at the appropriate point. Steep walking is well worth practising and if undertaken during a brisk effort a high pulse is easily maintained.

Race intensity hill reps

The intention of this session is to work hard, simulating the demands of racing itself. This must be done in a deliberate, controlled fashion. Too many athletes give themselves this type of work intensity 'accidentally', usually hanging-on on club nights, and line up tired for races. The total climbing time is best kept to around 12-14 minutes only, with the length of effort between 30 sec - 1 min 30 sec. The shortness of the effort enables powerful climbing and the athlete rapidly comes under stress. **BUT even this session should not be attacked with maximum effort and motivation.**

This work can be done unproductively too hard, leaving the athlete with too great a recovery problem despite the relative shortness of the session. The recovery should be sufficient to maintain a similar repetition time.

Useful body indicators are **breathing** and **muscular reaction affecting style**. If

Wayne Brown (Dewsbury), Alan Life (Clayton) and Colin Moses (Bingley) demonstrating the need for hill reps.

breathing becomes a gasping for breath affair be warned, the athlete is probably over-doing it. Similarly, if normal running rhythm is falling apart because of 'tying up', too great an effort is being made. This is the type of work that should be done sparingly. Once per week is sufficient, and not within 2 days of having raced or within 2 days of a race to come.

Whether a hill session should be endurance based or of race intensity will depend upon several factors: the background endurance already developed by the athlete, the demands of other planned training around the day in question and the proximity and length of races:

- if the athlete is lacking in endurance background the session would usually be best used for endurance
- if the athlete is recovering within a day or two of a hard race it should also be endurance based
- a fit athlete could do one of each in a week - though one endurance session would suffice if racing successive weekends

If possible it is a good idea to use a **variety of hills** for repetition training: races contain a wide variety of hills. The coach can determine the needs of the athlete, whether it be for more medium slope speed or the greater strength of very steep climbing.

Descending

Descending is well worth practising. If left to racing alone the athlete is likely to feel very uncomfortable attempting steep, rough descents at speed.

Like other aspects of training, practising descending does not have to be done at race speed to gain benefit, useful as that might be. There are a variety of ways of incorporating this into training, from fast descents during otherwise steady runs to specific downhill repetition sessions. The latter could be done as part of the hill repetition sessions, but if this option is

Jean Rawlinson (Clayton le Moors) demonstrating the art of descending in the 3 Peaks Race.

Rough descents require practice too. Clive Wilson (Keswick) and Andrew Shelbourne (Barnsley) descending at Dalehead.

chosen a short recovery at the bottom of the hill will be necessary to enable recovery before the next climb.

Points to consider:

- varying the length of stride
- varying the lightness of foot plant
- looking several strides ahead of the foot plant
- experimenting on a variety of terrains with heel, flat foot, or toe first foot plant
- increase confidence by visualising yourself descending fast
- find a comfortable degree of lean for the slope - the steeper the more upright
- wear close fitting shoes with good grip
- consider strength exercises for legs and ankles
- don't run flat out to the top - save something for the descent
- be prepared for an insecure foot plant
- total concentration on underfoot terrain

Track training

Track training is not an option most fell runners will choose. However, the serious fell aspirants would do well to consider this as an element in their programme. The advantage of track work is the speed at which intervals can be run. Many fell runners are in danger of never practising running fast in training. The consequence of that is they always feel lost for speed in short to medium fell races and uncomfortable when they try to run fast. For much of the season a top class fell runner might do one track repetition session and one hill session per week. To maximise the point of going on to the track it would usually be best to keep the session relatively short and intense, i.e. fast. 'Classic' 5K sessions should form the core: for example, 12 x 400m with about 1 min recovery, 6 x 800m with around 2 min recovery. The way to interpret the session would be as for the short hill repetition session.

The track can be used for other types of work, of course, such as a less intense speed practice session; for example, a brisk 12 x 300m with 100m jog, deliberately running with controlled rhythm which is not too intense but nonetheless fast.

Alternatives for off-road enthusiasts might be to transfer this type of work onto paths, trails, parks or playing fields. For the purposes of fell racing it is likely that just as useful work can be done on these terrains - and with less injury risk.

Other running

If an athlete trains according to the above, then other running must be carefully controlled also. Mostly, it needs to be **'recovery' running**. This is relaxed running, without pressure, to enable recovery from previous hard work and adequate freshness for the next hard session or race. The pace of this running will vary between athletes according to fitness and talent. Obvious as this is, it is worth stating as athletes commonly make the mistake of going for someone else's easy run, working too hard themselves.

A fit, talented athlete can run quite briskly and still be doing a recovery session, but even such an athlete should avoid pushing on recovery days. If in very good condition an occasional **light fartlek** session is as far as it ought to go. Getting this running 'wrong' will interfere with the quality of other planned hard work and can easily lead to fatigue, with the increased risk of injury or illness. Good class athletes can suffer at the hands of their less talented club mates if the latter are not motivated to do deliberate quality sessions, but attend club runs as alternatives to racing, pushing the former into working too hard.

Cross-training

Cross-training is doing a form of training different from the competition but with the aim of improving the latter. In concept it contradicts the main principle of adaptation, the **'principle of specificity',** which states that improvement in an activity is best gained by practising that activity, not alternatives. Cross-training depends upon **'transfer effect'** - the extent to which a different activity has a transfer benefit to the main activity.

Biking - an excellent alternative for the fell runner.

Mark Croasdale (Bingley) demonstrating another form of cross-training.

Arguably, running on the flat is cross-training for fell runners, whose main demands are up and down - though in fact few courses are literally 'up and down' only, and even those close to that definition have fast, runnable sections with medium slopes.

Other sports such as swimming or cycling are usually what come to mind when considering cross-training. They are often used at a time of running injury, or for a psychological break. But specific exercises, weight training and circuit training are further examples.

One of the advantages of specific exercises

is that particular muscle groups can be developed without interfering with the athlete's 'normal training' - provided the amount of work is sensibly controlled and does not leave the athlete sore or weary.

If activities are chosen instead of running, then those activities need to demand general endurance and muscular endurance of the legs, the thighs in particular. Otherwise the athlete's performance, despite some physical gains, is likely to deteriorate. The best alternative of this sort is **cycling** - road or off-road. Cycling not only makes the necessary aerobic demands but has the benefit, especially valuable to the fell runner, of placing extra emphasis on the thigh muscles, that group of muscles of especial significance to climbing and descending.

Andy Styan (Holmfirth) with the well developed quadriceps muscles of the conditioned fell runner.

A further advantage of cycling is that it is **non-impact** and so work loads can more readily be absorbed and the activity can be utilised for the full range of training purposes, from steady aerobic work to high intensity interval work. A disadvantage is that it takes **longer** in the saddle to match the gains of a running session. But a well thought out programme of running plus cycling will produce as good a result on the fells as a running programme alone.

Andy Peace and Ian Holmes (Bingley) prolific, successful racers on the fell.

Specific exercises

As the **ankle joint** comes under constant pressure from the uneven terrain of fell running it warrants particular attention. As a short term measure, if only to increase confidence, an athlete who is concerned about going over on weak ankles could make use of taping. Correctly done, taping lends strength to the joint without impeding its movement for the purposes of the race. But it is not a long term solution.

Strength is gained, of course, through fell running itself but complementary exercises would entail pointing, pulling, turning in and out, and rotating - all with a weight attached to the foot. Avoid undue stretching as 'slack' ligaments will add to the instability of the joint which wants to be firm and mobile but neither rigid nor slack.

Fell racing and training, hill reps and biking will all develop the **quadriceps,** but exercises such as half squats with weights, multigym leg presses, squat thrusts and step-ups are examples of worthwhile 'extras', especially for those living in fairly flat terrain. A more demanding extension of these activities are the more dynamic **plyometric** exercises such as hopping, leaping and drop jumps. Such exercises should be undertaken with care, after careful warm up, as they can easily result in injury. However, they do have the advantage of moving more specifically to the actual demands of fell racing.

Of the quadriceps muscles the **vastus medialis** on the front inside of the thigh warrants special attention. This muscle is readily left with comparative weakness to the others, and that weakness will result in an imbalance which all too readily leads to knee injury. To rectify this potential problem the leg should be exercised primarily in a straight leg position with the knee locked and the toes pulled toward the body. This exercise can be used as a therapeutic as well as a preventative measure. Not all knee problems relate to this muscle, of course, and any persistent pain should be referred to proper medical opinion.

The **hamstrings** at the back of the thigh can easily be neglected, and although they do not have to be as strong as the quadriceps they should not be neglected in any supplementary exercise programme. Although a hamstring curl station on a multi-gym is the commonest way of exercising this part of the body, an entirely acceptable alternative is to carry out the same movement with partner resistance around the ankle.

Although **maximum** strength, or gross strength, is best developed by the use of barbells or stacked weights in multigyms, the value of using **body weight** should not be under-estimated, especially by fell runners. A well designed **circuit training** programme (see Appendix 2) can be most beneficial, especially if the athlete experiences difficulty in maintaining the planned amount of running. Provided that heart rate is maintained at the appropriate level throughout the exercise, an aerobic effect can be attained for the duration of the activity in addition to strength gain.

Doing many sets and reps at loadings representing 75-85% of the performer's one rep maximum will tend to build bulky muscle. In some instances this may be desirable, but this is unlikely for most fell runners since that extra weight has to be carried. Strength training using loadings close to maximum (90% +) has been shown to improve strength with very little weight gain. This is attractive to fell runners and to fell running coaches. Those fell runners who have dabbled with strength training in the past have tended to go for relatively light weight and move it many times, e.g. 2 to 3 sets of 10 to 20 repetitions. This structure develops strength endurance, not power. Current thinking now inclines towards the type of strength training which put the yielding strength in to the frame of triple jumper Jonathan Edwards and took him beyond 18m. The same yielding strength is needed by fell runners when descending. That strength has been developed through lifting loads close to, or at maximum, and it has involved minimal (2lb) weight gain over 5 years. Few total lifts need to be made, e.g. 3 sets of 3 reps., or 6 sets of 1 rep. This can include back squats which are appropriate for fell runners. Full recovery (4-5 mins) is needed between each set. Weight training should be undertaken with expert guidance. Proper care should be taken over warm-up and technique before significant effort is made.

Clare Croft (Dark Peak) and Angela Brand-Barker, successful fell and international mountain runners over many years.

Racing

Many fell runners **over-race**, by the standards of other endurance runners. What appears strange to the non-fell runner is that this over-racing often appears to be carried out with impunity - fell runners get away with it, even seem to thrive on it. It would appear that the variety and typical softness of the terrain, and the more localised demands on parts of the body, enable the fell runner to more readily recover than the track or road runner racing

Fell racing poses a variety of hazards. Chris Beesley and Bill Hallahan (Horwich) crossing Hayeswater Gill during the Ian Hodgson Mountain Relay.

'Running the Gauntlet' in the Howarth Hobble '92. Just one of the hazards in this 33 mile race.

a similar length of time. Many fell runners start the season very unfit, race every week and gradually improve. Road or track runners attempting the same would be likely to injure or become ill. However, because such a regime is possible does not make it desirable or the **most productive** plan of development. One of the risks with this strategy is that runners can fool themselves into thinking there is no limit to the amount of racing their body can absorb and so race several times in a week. This is a high risk strategy no matter what the race results. After such exertions the athlete is highly prone to picking up infection or injury and possibly ruining the rest of the season.

A better plan is the more conventional approach of breaking the year up into **phases of 6-8 weeks** followed by an easy/rest week and planning minor races as stepping stones to target races. There are many possible patterns of varying work load over time, but a narrow interpretation of the concept of **'periodisation'** does not readily fit the racing year, or the typical psychology, of most fell runners. This is not to decry the value of base conditioning and peaking in key competitive periods, but for most these will be represented by only minor shifts in training and racing programmes at any one time in the year.

These and other matters should be given more consideration, of course, in the case of those seeking **international representation,** especially if they hope to perform with distinction in the **Trials** for and the **World Trophy** itself.

Footnote
The informality and low profile of fell running has been actively encouraged by its runners whose camaraderie has developed through an awareness of racing in a mountainous environment where help is sometimes more important than competition.

CHAPTER 5

Young Athletes

A great deal has been written about young athletes and the harmful effects that too much training and racing can have on their bones. Coaches today are ever more mindful of this problem, and fell running is no exception to the other disciplines. If racing is carefully monitored, and training down-hill is restricted, fell running with its soft underfoot running can allow a young athlete to develop with minimum risk of injury.

Children have been running and competing in fell races for many years. The village fairs and gala meetings in some parts of the country have encouraged games and sports of many kinds and, with their low key approach and emphasis on fun, they have been helpful in bridging the gap between track and cross country for those young athletes who enjoy all forms of running.

Enthusiasm for the sport of fell running increased so much, that by 1992 the FRA introduced additional age groups for the English Junior Championships; U12, U14 and U16, were added to the U18 and U20's. Each championship is currently based on the best four results from six designated races. Race distances vary from about 1 mile for the U12s, to 4 miles for the U16s. Safety standards are rigorously applied with race routes vetted and agreed safety requirements adhered to.

Training

A young athlete of 15 or under can undertake runs over rough terrain similar to a good cross country course, but planned interval work at those ages as described earlier for adults is **inappropriate**.

Athletes of all ages, of course, need to be reasonably conditioned for the event in which they take part. Running 2 or 3 times per week for aerobic conditioning, and not too far, should be sufficient alongside school sports activities.

A short fell race every couple of weeks with a grassy downhill descent will do no harm to the growing child.

About the age of 15, young fell runners are ready to embark upon specific ascending and descending practice. Before doing this they should undergo an assessment by their fell running coach.

Athletes fortunate enough to have had individual attention, and who have progressed through school events or track work, and so developed a good overall fitness and conditioning, are best placed to undertake more demanding workloads. Certainly between the ages of 17 to 19, young athletes with serious aspirations need to increase the regularity of training, and with a sound endurance base, insert some of the quality work, albeit reduced in

Victoria Wilkinson (Bingley) leading young athletes up Burnsall Fell.

volume, expected of good class senior athletes.

However, coaches have a responsibility for all children in their care and if in doubt should err on the side of caution, even to the extent of advising against the wishes of over enthusiastic parents. Besides the immediate concerns of the child, the coach should be looking to the sport, retaining interest, with many youngsters staying on to become senior fell runners, of whatever standard.

IMPORTANT

Because of the risk from injury in the growing child, every effort should be made to find a qualified coach to monitor their individual training programme. Information can be obtained through BAF or the FRA on those coaches qualified in the discipline of fell running.

CHAPTER 6

Mountain Marathons

This aspect of fell running and orienteering is extremely popular, with entries usually over-subscribed. The Karrimoor Mountain Marathon with standards to suit all levels of runners is considered to be the largest, in terms of entries, and possibly the most demanding, in that its October date can test both runner and equipment to their limit. The venue is changed each year and is kept secret to prevent runners reconnoitering the area.

The challenge of running for two days in mountainous terrain, carrying a rucksack with equipment required for an overnight camp, would seem a daunting and discouraging feat for most individuals, but year after year these same runners return to meet the challenge once again, and enjoy the companionship of running with a partner, that makes this type of event unique in the fell calendar.

Fully equipped and ready to go.
Derek Ratcliffe and Martin Stone.

Preparation

- Fitness
- Navigation
- Equipment
- Food and Drink

Fitness

The long Sunday run of two or three hours has its place, but a gradual increase in mileage must lead to extended periods of running that would equate with the expected daily mileage in the event. To focus on runs of this duration the ideal is to spend days in the Lake District or any other suitable mountainous location, and use the time running the fells with your partner, possibly checking over race routes that you intend to run later in the season.

Your rucksack should be gradually loaded so a true appreciation of the weight to be carried can be realised. The opportunity should be taken to eat and drink on the run, and certainly take time to practise navigational techniques. If an overnight camp at the side of a tarn can also be included in the outing, then valuable information can be gained on the equipment used, and the food to be eaten at the overnight camp. An occasional training run in inclement weather is also good preparation. Time spent over rough terrain is a better measure of preparation than 'road miles' or training on good paths. Clear guidelines are usually given in the pre-race information to indicate how long you can expect to be out running. Do not be over-ambitious in your choice of which course to run. A sensible decision, based on current fitness, can lead to an enjoyable weekend.

Navigation

Correct route choice plays a major part in deciding the winners, and for the lesser mortals how long they will be out. If the weather is adverse with limited visibility, especially in non-descript terrain, then intermediate runners can usually excel if their navigational skills are of the highest order. If the weather is fine and clear, then over the longer distances such as in the "A" and Elite Standard, then quality distance fell runners come into their own. This is a generalisation as there are some excellent runners who specialise in orienteering and some fell runners with equally good navigational skills.

Maps

Take the opportunity to have the map covered, either by ordering it covered or doing the job yourself. Nothing can be more frustrating than a gradually deteriorating map in rainy conditions. Also make sure that a waterproof marker pen is available for the map. It is also important to practise on a scale of map that you will be using in the race. The map is usually 1:40,000, i.e. 25mm (one inch) to one kilometre; the contour interval is 15 metres. This scale of map is available from past events, covering many areas.

On starting the event, and after collecting

Mike Parsons of Karrimor and partner sorting out route choice.

your description sheet, there is a tendency to be hasty in finding the first control point on the map, as runners around you are leaving the area. This temptation should be avoided. An extra minute spent ensuring a correct route choice can pay dividends later. Don't make the mistake of guessing that the couple in front are in your standard and be tempted to follow. Some runners like to mark the map with all the controls before continuing; others take the first one and go, marking later controls as they proceed. The choice depends on experience. Double checking of map references can pay dividends, with both runners involved! Leaving all the navigation decisions to one runner can sometimes prove costly, and allows a valuable learning situation to be wasted.

Equipment

There is no doubt that having good light equipment can make the difference between continued running, as opposed to extended periods of walking. With the right equipment and food, your rucksack should weigh in at approximately 12-15 lb (4.5-6.8kg). Some use lighter packs if anticipated weather conditions allow, but in general, if the weight is kept within a couple of pounds of this range a considerable advantage can be gained over other runners with heavier packs.

John Gibbison (FRA Navigation Course Tutor) and partner putting theory into practice.

Tent

The tent is one of the two major items of weight, and if money is no object then considerable savings can be made with today's ultra lightweight models of approximately 3 lb. (1.3 kg). Some runners like their comfort and space, and pay for the privilege in weight.

Sleeping Bag

This is the second heaviest item and must be capable of doing the job for which it is intended. Even on a fine day, after a day's exertions on the fells the body rapidly cools once stationary, and a warm bag is essential. Some runners do not carry a change of clothing and the sleeping bag has both to warm up the runner and dry the clothes before morning. Lightness (approximately 2-3 lb. (1-1.3kg) for a 3-4 seasons bag) is desirable, but depending on anticipated weather conditions you must have a sleeping bag that gives you the warmth and comfort for a good night's sleep.

Sleep Mat

Whether to have the comfort of one under the sleeping bag is a personal choice. Some can't sleep without one, others don't require one. The thin bubble sheeting that is used for packaging can be used as an alternative.

Rucksack

Your sack has to be your friend for two days and its comfort can go a long way in maintaining your enthusiasm for continued effort, so buy carefully and ask around before buying. Basic requirements are: padded shoulder straps, good chest straps to stop bounce, waterproof and light (about 300 grams) and with external netting or mini pockets for odd things on the run. Even if waterproof, it is advisable to line the inside with a plastic bin liner as extra protection for dry clothes.

Stove

The stove must be reliable and light (around 145 grams plus gas) and there is no substitute for using it time and again in practice, preparing the food you will eat at the overnight camp. Detail, like checking the flame time for all your requirements, can allow you to minimise the quantity of gas taken. If you extend this level of detail to all your equipment then considerable savings on weight can be achieved .

Preparing for day two at the overnight camp.

Torch

An item of equipment that a runner hopes not to use before the overnight camp, but in reality those fortunate enough to be in the warmth of their tent, watching a line of flashing torches in the dark on the fell side, know only too well they too could have needed a good torch to get safely into camp. Make sure that the batteries are new and a spare bulb is carried. Head torches are handy, but some runners still prefer hand torches.

Clothing

Again personal choice prevails, but a runner must be prepared for bad weather, and items like good gloves and balaclava are essential. Thermal gear is the basis of a runner's kit, and leg cover is a necessity. The event instructions on what should be carried must be adhered to. If the forecast is for bad weather, then consideration should be given for fully waterproof material like Gortex. Although weight conscious runners may opt for the lighter rip stop nylon, even with thermal underclothing hypothermia cannot be ruled out in adverse conditions. Once again it is the testing of suitable clothing in bad weather on long Sunday runs that gives one the experience to know what is required.

Food and Drink

It goes without saying that a carbo rich diet a few days before the event helps considerably on the first day, and a sensible

Andy Schofield (Borrowdale) ready for the evening meal.

breakfast before the start sets the day off right. If you are booked for an early start then be cautious with too big a breakfast; there may be insufficient time to digest it. The previous evening meal and supper is more of a priority. During the event powdered carbohydrate drinks are sufficient to supply the energy required for most runners (although some do feel the need to eat something filling), helped with a favourite running snack to keep up morale. Keeping well hydrated is essential, especially if sweating heavily. Your condition when you arrive at the overnight camp site usually determines what course of action is taken next. Arriving in good weather, in daylight, and feeling fine, gives you the option of having a snack, possibly soup, and drink before pitching the tent. But for those who arrive after 8 hours or more, sometimes in the dark feeling possibly the worse for wear, pitching the tent and getting inside can be crucial. It is certainly important to eat and drink something as soon as is practicable, but not all runners who have given their all can stomach food before they have had a rest, or indeed a nap.

Evening Meal

This is a personal choice with an array of favourites usually on view at the overnight camp. The basis should be that of dehydrated foods. Potato flakes, rice or pasta, mixed with a dry soya meat with water added, will give a full and satisfying meal. A dessert of rice, with dried banana slices topped with instant mixed custard, makes a suitable sweet. Consuming enough water is essential. Check the colour of your urine; if it is dark in colour much water needs to be drunk.

Supper

If the evening meal is taken early it can be a long time before finally going to sleep, so a cup of hot chocolate with a few biscuits can fill that gap.

Breakfast

A good breakfast would be a large helping of porridge oats. Prepare the oats, powdered milk, salt and sugar to taste, all in one bag before the event so it is ready for the boiling water.

NOTE: THE FOOD ITEMS INDICATED HAVE BEEN USED SUCCESSFULLY, BUT IT IS YOUR PERSONAL CHOICE THAT MATTERS. DO NOT WAIT UNTIL THE EVENT TO TRY THEM OUT.

Second Day

This is usually shorter than the first, and a snack after two or three hours will usually be sufficient before the finish. Variations from marzipan, to lumps of currant cake, to figs and dates, have all been used en route. Do take the trouble in training to establish what you like to eat on the run. Some runners find that they can only drink, so carbo drinks are all that is taken. Always try to follow the formula of consuming something every hour to stay topped up.

Don't forget the mini treats at camp like the chocolate chip cookies to snack on, or the powdered orange drink that eases your thirst where water at times can be bland. Extra energy with Kendal Mint Cake or Dextrasol provide a good back up.

Tips

- Check **each other's** kit before the start, and share the weight evenly (unless not evenly paired).
- Do not start the event with too much clothing on; you soon get warm!
- Eliminate all rattles in the sack before starting the event.
- Keep small plastic bags with carbo-powder available whilst running, for filling at streams.
- Try to eat a little every hour when running; don't wait until it is too late.
- Put on your waterproofs as you arrive at the overnight camp.
- Small candles can save the torch battery in camp.
- Thermal long johns can be a boon at the camp, with spare thermal top.
- Bubble pack sleeping mats can be discarded (in bin provided) after camp.
- Large plastic bags for storing water (ex-wine container with tap).
- Small plastic bags for the feet to keep spare socks dry.
- Windproof, waterproof matches are a must at times.
- Pot noodle containers are useful for other dishes, but are bulky to carry.
- Plastic mugs and tinfoil plates all help to keep the weight down.
- One large plastic spoon serves all requirements (watch the heat in the cooking tin).
- Keep down sleeping bags dry in the tent - or suffer extra weight during the second day.
- Dry toilet paper is a must; be prepared for a communal toilet!

Competitors contending with severe weather.

Pre-race enthusiasm and enjoyment starts with kit preparation, so plan early. Those who leave this task to the last minute can sometimes have a disappointing weekend due to the omission of some item of equipment.

3 Peaks Yacht Race

Fell running can also be linked with other sports as in the 3 Peaks Yacht Race. This venture which started back in 1977 requires much more planning than even the Mountain Marathons with the requirement of a good yacht and crew, five in all, including the runners. The race starts from Barmouth. The first port of call is Caernarfon, where the runners disembark for the run to the top of Snowdon and back. This procedure is repeated at Ravenglass with the scaling of Scafell, and finally up the coast to Fort William and the final run up and down Ben Nevis. The knack is to co-ordinate the times of the runners with those of the tides, and of course having good navigation from the yacht crew as well as the runners. This can be a real adventure, with rough seas at times making great demands on both yacht and crew. There have been incidents much more unpleasant than the expected dose of sea sickness. The winning time can be completed in around 2-3 days, weather permitting, but back markers can take up to a week. The total running time is around 11-12 hours for those up front.

3 Peaks Yacht Race. Add team spirit, sailing and adventure to running the fells, and you have a memorable event.

Fell Running on the Islands

For those intending a holiday in Ireland or the Isle of Man, take your fell shoes with you. The FRA fixtures calendar is sprinkled with races of all standards. The Manx Mountain Marathon at Easter weekend with 30 miles and 8000 feet of climbing is certainly a challenge. Needless to say, the Scottish Isles also have races to savour such as Goatfell to the Bens of Jura.

On the final climb of the Bens of Jura race.

Fell Running Abroad

Fell running is not just the prerogative of the British; there is a full calendar of events abroad. Races are in abundance on the continent with many British fell runners enjoying the hospitality of our European friends. One of the most popular races on the continent is the Sierre-Zinal race. At 31k long with 2000m of climb this race is full of character and charisma. The hospitality of the Swiss is superb and the little village of Zinal, with its carnival atmosphere at the finish, makes the race an holiday event. The race caters for all standards, with a special section for those who walk the course, but they must be prepared to start early at 5am!

John Nixon (Horwich), a regular competitor on the continent, here amidst the magnificent scenery of the Matterhorn.

CHAPTER 7

Training and Racing Guidelines for International Mountain Competition

World Trophy courses

International mountain racing is significantly unlike British Category 'A' fell racing. Although parts of courses may be very severe, the proportion of severe ascent is usually much less than is to be found in Britain. One consequence of this is that much of an international course is likely to consist of fast running gradients or even lengthy flat stretches. But of even greater significance is the typical difference in descent. Many international races have no descent - they are climbs only. The most important event on the calendar, the World Trophy, is in continuous dispute on this point, sometimes offering climbs and descent, at other times climbs only. Taking this into account, the FRA has used the varied but often fast terrain between Keswick, Latrigg and Skiddaw for selection purposes.

Important training and racing consequences follow from the above. If talented athletes consider they are essentially fell runners and train and race on the fells only, fitting in 'having a go' at the Trials, they may well not make the team, and if they do they are likely to be lost for speed at the World event. There are problems in both the training and racing programmes of the above approach.

The athletes could be faced with never running as fast in either training or racing as they need to try and do in the Trial or Championship race. This has an immediate and striking effect in the key race as they feel very uncomfortable trying to move that quickly and rapidly 'tie up' because they are not conditioned to the intensity. However, few top class fell runners with international potential are likely to find themselves quite that ill prepared as they are likely to do some sort of varied pace training and will compete in short, fast fell races. Although their speed training could well benefit from more precision, a much more common problem for such athletes is an inappropriate racing programme.

Risks of over-racing

Fit fell runners are notorious over-racers. They love competing in whatever happens to be on next weekend, and often mid-week too. Some have been known to race several times in the space of 7 days with considerable success. But if they look back over the season they are likely to find that the same period was their 'purple patch' and race performances slipped thereafter. Once conditioned to the fells, the fit athlete can race more frequently than would otherwise be possible on road, track or cross-country. But that does not mean it is a good idea to do so. A far safer way to ensure progress is to select races carefully and use the opportunity for greater control offered by hard training to develop racing potential. In particular the number of long races in a season should be very cautiously planned. An annual problem for the keen fell runner who would also like to compete in the World Trophy is the fell championship racing demands of the season. This is particularly problematic if the athletes aim for both their home country championship as well as the British. It is well nigh impossible to do themselves justice with all three targets. Aiming for all three, disappointment is likely to follow somewhere. An athlete aiming for the World Trophy and still wishing to go for the championships ought to decide on one championship only, and also be prepared to miss the odd event should best preparation demand it.

World Trophy

Final phase preparation

Quite apart from preparing for international events early season, specific preparation for the Trial should start at least 6 weeks before the event. This assumes that the athlete is in very good condition at that time and has not by then raced to a point of persistent slight fatigue, or worse. From that point in time the keen fell runner should not consider racing any Long fell races of whatever category, and would be well advised to avoid the longer Medium races. The best racing strategy would be to select 'B' or 'C' races in preparation for the target races. It must also be borne in mind that the 'A' races carry a greater risk of injury. A badly sprained ankle at the height of the season can be very frustrating. However, fell runners like racing the fells

John Taylor, Matthew Moorhouse and Mark Kinch representing England in the World Trophy at Edinburgh.

and so races should be largely confined to Short events, preferably shorter in time than the 'Trial' race and the World event. For those prepared to step off the fell, an even more productive racing preparation would include, and would already have included, races on road and track. Races on road or track should also be 'short'. The obvious advantage of racing road or track is the much higher speed practised. But that advantage is wasted if the 'wrong' events are chosen. Races longer than 10K on the road should not form part of the programme at any time during the summer, and certainly not in the 6 weeks prior to the 'Trial' or the World Trophy.

Longer road or fell races not only demand considerable recovery but interfere with the training preparation that could otherwise be done. Even 10K road races should be used very sparingly. Similarly, track races are best confined to 3000m/5000m events, not 10,000m. It must be emphasised, however, that 'flat' racing alone is not a good idea for the last 6-8 weeks as both 'Trial' and World Trophy courses demand intense climbing. Although tough hill reps can prepare in part for this, racing over such gradients is even more valuable preparation.

Many athletes ignore these guidelines and some appear to do quite well. But could they have done significantly better? We'll never know, but the above principles are in the best interests of the vast majority and we should be careful quoting the exceptional individual as a prescription for the majority.

Tommy Murray (Scotland), an elite runner over all terrains and Silver Medalist at Edinburgh '95.

Athletes of a non-fell background

Increasingly World Trophy teams and international mountain competitors come from either a non-fell background or at least a wider variety of athletic backgrounds than fell running alone. It by no means automatically follows that top class 5000m/10,000m track, road and cross-country performers will make good mountain racers, still less good fell racers. But it's a good start. As with all disciplines, elite performers are the result of innate ability plus consistent, specific training. Many fast flat runners are not good 'natural' climbers and if they wish to become so must train for it. The most obvious way of training for it is to do repetition or sustained climbs - if long enough ones are available.

Broad training principles

There is no one way, one 'magic schedule', for training but one thing all consistently top class athletes have in common is the motivation to apply themselves to a considerable volume of work over a significant period of time. Training in a non-mountainous locality, senior international aspirants need to think of about 70 miles per week upwards. This equates to an average of about an hour's good running training per day as a minimum. Any less volume and the athlete is unlikely to develop the endurance base from which high level, consistent race performances follow and is unlikely to realise full potential. Few runners will spend the same amount of time training each day, but vary training according to a convenient weekly pattern or other time unit. The length of time spent training is a useful measure for those training in a mountainous environment as a similar workload can be achieved over much less mileage. However, few athletes are likely to train daily on hills, partly because of their demands and partly because of the increased injury risk, to the knees in particular. Also it is good to learn how to run fast on the flat.

Andy Peace (Helwith Bridge Alers) in the 3 Peaks Cyclo Cross showing one can mix fell and bike.

Biking, on road or off road, is an increasingly popular alternative which, because of its specific demands on the thigh muscles, is of particular benefit to mountain runners. Biking has two further advantages: it carries less injury risk and enables faster recovery than does running. To gain full advantage from it the serious athlete should make a deliberate, planned use of biking, not simply 'ride to work' now and again, though that can be a convenient part of bike training. A serious use means knowing when the bike is being used for recovery work, good quality aerobic work or race conditioning work and planning that usage alongside running training. The main disadvantage of biking is that it usually takes a good deal more time in the saddle to achieve the work loads gained by running. Other forms of cross-training are worth exploring but few will produce the same benefits as biking for the runner, the mountain runner in particular.

Planning a training and racing programme

A sensible training programme can only be worked out in relation to the racing programme of which it is a part. The whole is best broken down into different periods of the year with their different emphases - what the text books call 'periodisation'. It pays to plan the occasional easy week after perhaps 6-8 weeks good quality training. Some prefer a pattern of 'easy' to 'medium hard' to 'hard' weeks and other combinations which enable recovery from hard work. Whatever the pattern, the ambitious athlete needs to decide on key targets and gear training and racing programmes to those ends. This carries a major risk. If the key targets do not come off the athlete can be left feeling very deflated. They alone know whether it is worth it. Although it is motivating to have targets throughout the year, an athlete aiming primarily at mountain racing mid to late summer should regard the winter as a period of preparation and conditioning. Racing, including target races, would properly form part of the winter - but not too frequently. Racing week after week will ultimately have a destructive effect, not a building effect.

There would be little point in the ambitious mountain racer starting the spring or early summer jaded from over-racing. The selective winter racing programme could happily consist of cross-country, fell, road or bike racing. But almost all of these races should be taken within a fairly normal volume of training. Too frequent sharpening up or cutting back for races will interfere with overall development. But this does not mean racing tired. Racing tired is not only bad for morale but carries an increased risk of injury and is destructive of the training which follows. The way to 'train through races' and still race well is to reduce the intensity of some of the work in the preceding week in particular.

Robin Bergstrand (Mandale), one of England's most consistent athletes.

Training sessions and their purposes

It is possible to run very well by doing continuous running all the time and training 'as you feel', but working to a planned week with deliberate hard sessions and deliberate easy runs is far more likely to produce the best result. In a typical training week, with no race at the end, the fit athlete should be trying to complete 3 good quality sessions. Two of those could be intermittent running, one on the flat, one on hills, and one continuous hard. It is a good idea to vary the elements in a session, if only for psychological reasons and although there are a 101 possible combinations, a useful pattern is:

- One of the intermittent sessions could consist of long repetitions such as 4 or 5 x 5 min., with about a 2-3 min recovery jog after each effort.
- Another intermittent session could be shorter in effort and total volume, but faster e.g. 12 x 1 min with 1 min jog recovery.
- The sustained run, over undulating terrain, could be anything from 3 to 10 miles.

The long rep session should be run at a 'good, hard pace'. Although this appears a rather unscientific description, the pace tends to take care of itself because of the size of the session. Aiming to run a fairly even pace, an athlete starting too fast soon feels the need to slow down. Another subjective indicator is for the athlete to think of about 10K racing pace and rhythm for the speed and intensity of the efforts. With the benefit of a heart rate monitor the aim is to be a little bit below the zone in which lactates start to accumulate rapidly, causing undue recovery needs. If this session is to be a hill session the athlete must be very careful not to work too hard. The pace feels very slow on anything above a slight gradient, and would probably have to drop to a brisk walk on very steep sections to stay within the training intentions of the session. Steep walking is well worth practising for mountain racers. Similarly, brisk descending needs to be practised at some time in the athlete's week.

The intentions of the short rep session are quite different. Not only is the practice of speed an important purpose, but this is a race intensity conditioning session. It is meant to be hard, conditioning the body to the high lactates experienced in races typical of 'short' and 'medium' fell races. But hard does not mean flat out. A teeth-gritting affair will leave the athlete with too great a recovery burden despite the relatively small size of the session. The fairly short jog interval deliberately prevents full recovery between efforts. A useful subjective indicator is to run as fast as possible whilst keeping the same sense of rhythm and control throughout.

The intention of the continuous hard run is similar to that of the long rep session but with the added psychological demand of keeping going. The length of the run can be usefully varied according to the needs of the time of year. In an important competitive period it can get a little nearer

the competitive intensity of racing by keeping it short. But unless the session is used as a substitute for the short rep session it is important to hold back a little from actual race intensity. As a mountain racer it is better to do this session over hilly or mountainous terrain than on the flat.
In a race week the race becomes the intense session. The safest training procedure therefore is to do the long rep session, possibly slightly reduced. If the short rep session is also done, and it may be preferable to a steady run, it should be at much reduced intensity, becoming more of a racing rhythm session. Working harder risks lining up tired for the race.

Martin Jones.

Carol Greenwood.

All other mileage needs to be run cautiously. Its aims are recovery from the hard work and the building of general endurance. It is possible for the very fit athlete to do one or two light fartlek sessions on these days, running fast and slow, never flat out and with good recoveries. Alternatively, the pace could be lifted to a 'good steady' continuous run. But the session should never become a hard one and should switch to easy running if obviously tired. Just because it is easy, athletes should not neglect or undervalue this running as without it the development they will get from the quality work will be severely limited and short lived. If they look to get too much quality out of any of this running they are likely to become too tired to do the planned quality sessions correctly.

It must be appreciated that the above training suggestions can only be adopted and adapted by athletes who are already quite fit. In this context 'quite fit' means able simply to run a steady 70 miles per week, or its equivalent, with relatively little effort.

The Training Programmes of Two Former World Trophy Champions

Martin Jones

Typical week in 1992

Mon.	a.m. 45 min cycling	p.m. 35 min steady running
Tues.	a.m. 45 min cycling	p.m. 10 x 800 m, 30 sec recovery
Wed.	a.m. 45 min cycling	p.m. 50 min steady
Thur.	a.m. 45 min cycling	p.m. 10 x hill, 1 min hard up & hard down
Fri.	a.m. 45 min cycling	p.m. 35 min steady
Sat.	a.m. 45 min cycling	p.m. 7 miles hard
Sun.	1 hr 30 min over the moors	

The repetition work was preceded by a good warm up and followed by a good cool down. Martin says his cycling made him significantly faster running uphill but emphasises that the cycling was done at a good pace, not an easy ride. He also feels the frequency of it is very important. However, in 1993, when Martin retained his title, he had started track racing and substituted the cycling with a 30 min easy run each morning, except Sun. Although he did some hill rep work, his final preparation for the World title race consisted of a month labouring and training in the Lake District to better acclimatise his legs to the severity of the terrain. Prior to that month a typical week was:

Mon.	a.m. 30 min easy	p.m. 35 min steady
Tues.	a.m. 30 min easy	p.m. 12 x 400 m
Wed.	a.m. 30 min easy	p.m. 50 min steady
Thur.	a.m. 30 min easy	p.m. 10 x hill/medium gradient, 1 min hard up & hard down
Fri.	a.m. 30 min easy	p.m. 40 min steady
Sat.	a.m. 30 min easy	p.m. fartlek incorporating 6 x 3 min over fells
Sun.	1 hr 30 min steady over fells	

Although Martin usually trained twice a day, for an athlete of his standard the total work load might be thought to be relatively modest. However, two important points need to be borne in mind: firstly, consistent training such as the above is a very significant discipline over time which will produce results, as Martin demonstrated; secondly, Martin's 'easy' runs and 'steady' runs may well have been at a brisker pace than many might assume by those terms, i.e. his work load may well have been higher than the volume suggests.

CAROL GREENWOOD

Typical week's training

Mon.	a.m. 30 min easy	p.m. 12 x 400 m, 100 m jog recovery
Tues.	a.m. 30 min easy	p.m. 10 miles with club
Wed	a.m. 4-6 x 800 m, lap jog recovery	p.m. easy run or bike ride
Thur.	a.m. 30 min easy	p.m. 10 miles with club
Fri.	5 miles	
Sat.	Race	
Sun.	Race or 2hr run or bike ride	

As well as the above, Mon. - Fri. Carol would usually do a 30 min turbo cycle ride at lunch time and go for the occasional swim! During the summer of her championship win she raced track, road and fell.

Needless to say, Carol is renowned for her demanding work load and the frequent racing programme that it enabled her to absorb. It would be foolish to attempt to emulate this overnight, but all the ingredients for successful mountain racing are there for others to adapt.

Matthew Moorhouse leading the way in the World Trophy Junior event at Edinburgh.

APPENDIX 1

Organisation and Regulations

The British Athletic Federation

BAF was formed on 17th March, 1991, and is the governing body for the sport of athletics, of which Fell/Hill Running is a discipline in the U.K. The policies of BAF are determined by its General Meetings and by its Council, the members of which are widely representative of the sport. Fell/Hill Running has one seat on the Council.

The Fell and Hill Running Commission

The management of various disciplines of the sport for the United Kingdom and international affairs is undertaken by the Commissions of the Federation. The Fell and Hill Running Commission consists of members elected by the regional associations of fell/hill running as follows:

England - 3, Scotland - 2, Wales - 1, Northern Ireland - 1.

The chairman of the Fell and Hill Running Commission is elected from amongst their number by the commission members. The secretary is elected at the AGM of the BAF.

Regional Associations

BAF delegate the administration of athletics to the following regional bodies:
Northern Ireland A.A.F. Scottish A.F. A.A. of Wales
Midland Counties A.A. North of England A.A. South of England A.A.

The Fell/Hill running Regional Associations are:
England - The Fell Runners Association
Scotland - The Scottish Athletics Federation Hill Running Commission
Wales - The Welsh Fell Runners Association
Northern Ireland - The Northern Ireland Fell Runners Association

These Associations each have committees elected by the individual fell/hill running membership in their regions. They have a link with the BAF regional bodies which is parallel with their link to the commission.

The FRA is linked to the North of England A.A, the Scottish Athletics Federation Hill Running Commission to the Scottish Athletics Federation, the Welsh Fell Runners Association to the A.A. of Wales, and the Northern Ireland Fell Runners Association to the Northern Ireland A.A.F.

The fell/hill running associations nominate members to serve on the Fell/Hill Running Commission.

International

B.A.F. are affiliated to the International Amateur Athletic Federation which is the controlling body of athletics world-wide.

The position of Fell/Hill running at an international level is different from other forms of athletics in that the International Amateur Athletic Federation have not yet adopted this discipline as an integral part of world athletics.

Co-ordination of the sport at international level is undertaken by the International Committee for Mountain Running (I.C.M.R.). Each country is allowed one member to vote at the annual meeting of this committee. The International Committee for Mountain Running exercise no executive control over the annual "World Trophy Mountain Races".

The International Committee for Mountain Running liaise with the International Amateur Athletic Federation via the latter's Cross Country and Road Running Committee.

The International Committee for Mountain Running accepts, for historical reasons, that the United Kingdom is four separate countries - England, Northern Ireland, Scotland and Wales. These countries are permitted to enter teams in the World Trophy.

The I.A.A.F act as "patrons" to this committee. The I.A.A.F Rule Book recognises mountain running in Rule 167.10 which specifies the following recommended approximate distances and total amounts of ascent for international events.

Danny Hughes, President of ICMR 1994 - 97.

	Distance	Ascent
MAINLY UPHILL		
Senior Men	12km	1200m
Senior Women	7km	550m
Junior Men	7km	550m
START/FINISH AT SAME LEVEL		
Senior Men	12km	700m
Senior Women	7km	400m
Junior Men	7km	400m

Not more than 20% of the distance may be on tarmac road.

FRA Rules for Competition

DEFINITIONS

ONE – OFFICIAL FRA FELL RACE

An "official FRA fell race" is one held under FRA Rules for Competition and BAF Rules for Competition in so far as they concern fell-running.

TWO – RACE CATEGORIES

A fell race is run on fell, hill or mountain terrain and shall be categorised as follows:

CATEGORY "A"

- Should average not less than 250' climb/mile.
- Should not have more than 20% of the race distance on the road.
- Should be at least one mile in length.

CATEGORY "B"

- Should average not less than 125' climb/mile.
- Should not have more than 30% of the race distance on the road.

CATEGORY "C"

- Should average not less than 100' climb/mile.
- Should not have more than 40% of the race distance on the road.
- Should contain some genuine fell terrain.

THREE – RACE LENGTHS

Category 'L' (long) race twelve miles or over.
Category 'M' (medium) race six miles and over but under twelve.
Category 'S' (short) race under six miles.

FOUR – CLUBS

A "club" as referred to in the Rules indicates a club which is affiliated to the BAF or one of its constituent bodies. The FRA is a constituent body of the BAF and so "club" also refers to those clubs affiliated to the FRA.

Rules

The rules governing fell/hill races in England /Wales/Northern Ireland are those of the FRA - as published in the FRA Handbook. Scottish rules have developed independently but the Commission are in the process of unifying the rules for the whole of the U.K.

1 All "official FRA fell races" are those registered with the FRA. This registration shall be effected by supplying the Fixtures Secretary with the relevant details of the race on the form provided and by its subsequent appearance in the FRA Calendar or supplement or magazine. A charge is made to cover Calendar publication expenses and race insurance.

2 "Official FRA fell races" must be advertised and decided under the FRA and BAF Rules. Such advertisement may be abbreviated to read "under FRA Rules".

3 All competitors in "official FRA fell races" must be amateurs as defined by the BAF Rules for Competition.

4 All "official FRA fell races" must be organised to comply with the FRA Safety Requirements printed at the front of the Calendar, copies of which are obtainable from the Fixtures Secretary on receipt of a SAE.

5 All competitors must obey the FRA Rules for Competition and any additional Rules drawn up by the race organiser for each fell race in order to accommodate specific local routes or safety needs.

6 No runner may take part in any fell race without having entered the race in accordance with the rules and procedures.

7 All competitors must ensure that if they retire from a fell race for any reason the fact is reported as soon as possible to the race officials, including those at the finish. Race organisers MUST report infringements of this rule to the FRA Secretary.

8 Runners may count in competition for their first claim fell-running club only. This club may be different from their first claim road, cross-country or track club if that club does not cater for fell-running.

9 BAF Rules 3 and 4 (Club Membership and First Claim Status) apply to all clubs affiliated to BAF or the FRA. BAF Rule 4 requires a 9 months' waiting period between ceasing membership of a club and competing as a team member for another club.

Claims for exemption from this rule may be made to the appropriate BAF region except when either of the clubs involved is affiliated to the FRA only, in which case claims should be submitted to the FRA.

10 Race organisers must stipulate age limits for their events but the following lower age limits must apply to all events.

Under 12 years - 2 miles
Under 14 years - 3 miles
Under 16 years - 4 miles
Under 18 years - 6 miles

Ages are as at the 1st January in the year of competition.

The minimum age for competition under FRA Rules is 11 years on the day of the race.

11 The FRA executive committee is empowered to take whatever action is deemed necessary on a report in writing of the breach of any of these Rules by competitors or organisers at an "official FRA fell race".

There is a right of appeal to the BAF Fell and Hill Running Commission.

The following time scales shall be adhered to in any such process :

a) Notification shall be in writing to the FRA Secretary within fourteen days of the event in question.

b) The FRA executive shall investigate and conclude its findings and make a decision within seven weeks of the event in question.

c) Notification of the FRA decision will be given in writing to the parties concerned within eight weeks of the event in question.

The above are maximum time scales; the process should be expedited as rapidly as possible, hopefully in a briefer time-span than outlined above.

APPENDIX 2

Circuit Training

A good circuit training session is part of any well planned schedule. Like the stretch routines, ancillary exercises are essential in maintaining overall body fitness.

It does not require a well laid out gymnasium to have a successful circuit.

The following circuit contains all the ingredients of a well organized and tough circuit. This routine has been chosen to demonstrate how, with a little enthusiasm and ingenuity, anyone can put together a circuit for a small group of runners. For those fortunate enough to have more idyllic surroundings, the old adage of 'it's not what you've got, it's more what you do with it, that matters' applies here.

The principles of setting up a good circuit are seldom outlined in books. It is usually just the exercises that are shown in a photo or drawing, and the rest is left to you. The following is for those athletes and coaches who have yet to use a circuit.

- Ensure that each exercise has a variable intensity to accommodate differing degrees of fitness.
- Encourage those new to the circuit to take the first few sessions easy.
- Arrange the stages so that different muscle groups are worked as you move along.
- Arrange a time at each stage that works the athletes without demanding more than they can give.
- Suitable music with a regular beat optimizes the intensity.
- Arrange the stages so that one rep per beat is the norm, with perhaps two beats to one on difficult exercises.
- Ensure that the overall time for the circuit is stretching the athletes without draining them.
- Try to keep the temperature under control to prevent over-heating.
- Keep safety in mind when planning the various stages.
- Encourage everyone to exercise at a rate that also works them aerobically.
- Keep athletes away from stages that may aggravate current niggles!

There are circuits for all occasions. For example, super setting (maintaining an exercise intensity on one muscle group over several stages in succession) the stages to intensify work on a particular muscle group is one variation. Making certain stages with a slower tempo for muscle building emphasis can be another.

The permutations are endless. The one shown is a general circuit to work the upper body and stomach, with a little for the legs, but this can be extended or modified according to individual needs. The fell runner doing few or no hill reps. could add plyometric strength exercises such as hopping, leaping and bounding. But such demanding work should be done only when thoroughly warmed up. What is shown is a typical selection, not only to suit the athletes but to accommodate the space available.

Circuit Explanation

Number of Stages
Eight.

Time Values
Use of a count down facility on a watch is helpful. Set the watch at 50 sec repeat. Ten seconds is used to move from stage to stage, with 40 seconds actually working.

Number of circuits
Three to start, four as a norm, and five for those who are super fit.

The intensity of the circuit is helped considerably if suitable music provides a beat that focuses the attention and establishes a rhythm to work to. It also creates a conducive atmosphere for the group.

The correct **tempo beat** will give approximately 46 press ups in 40 seconds.

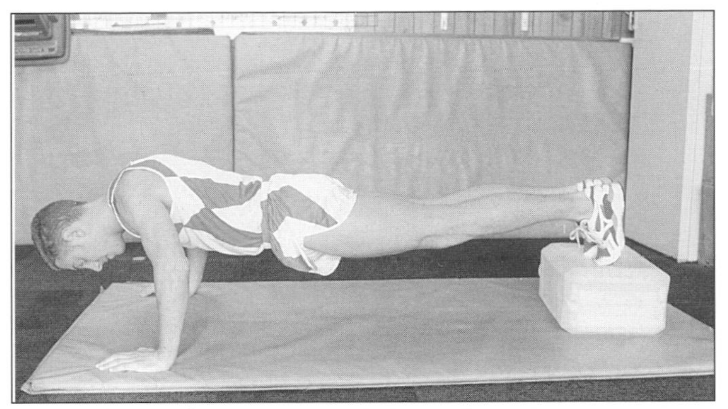

1. PRESS UPS

Press ups have a three option stage. For those who can do fifty plus, use a box for the feet to create an inclined press. For those in the 10 to 30 group, no box is required, just straight forward press ups, arms slightly wider than shoulder width. For those not used to press ups, then the knees should rest on the floor at varying angles so that the stage time is completed with effort. One press up, one beat.

2. SIT UPS

Either: Maintain a constant pressure on the stomach muscles by describing a small arc in doing the exercise, neither lying fully back nor sitting fully up. Or: For the more demanding work and the ambitious handy man, construct an inclined board. An old ladder is convenient cut down to size. A seven foot padded board, covered with carpet oddments with two metal hooks on the end to grip over the rungs, is great for a quick adjustment. A suitable strap is required at the end for the feet to hold under. The ladder has to be solidly fixed to a good support. Keep the legs bent on the board and raise the trunk, with the hands preferably at the side of your head to eliminate possible neck problems when tired - through pulling too hard. The position of the arms and how they are worked in the sit up can vary the effort needed considerably, and moving the ladder up or down on the rungs is another way. One sit up - two beats.

3. SINGLE LEG SQUAT THRUSTS

This is similar to running in a start position. The degree of effort required is governed by how far the legs are brought forward and moved back, the larger the stride the harder the effort. Very easy to maintain stride with music beat. Keep arms wider than shoulder width. One stride one beat. Those super fit may like to try the full two leg squat thrusts, one rep to two beats.

4. LEG CIRCLES

A great exercise for the abductors and adductors. Place an object, chair or box in front of you and circle the legs in an outward rotational movement. This means setting the right leg off over the left side of the object in a clockwise direction, lightly touch the floor before next circle. One set of 24 per leg is about right. The height of the obstacle to lift the leg over regulates the intensity. One circle to a beat is difficult, two beats the norm.

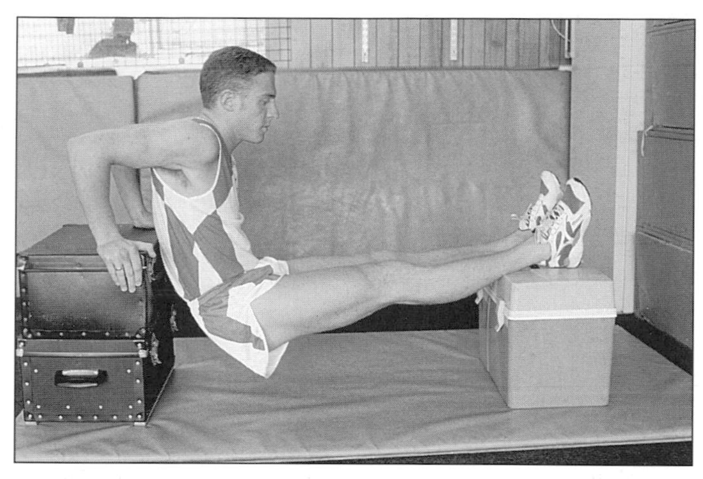

5. TRICEPS DIPS

The harder set is with the legs raised on a box or chair. The easier way is with the feet on the floor. Place a secure box or object behind you and with your hands in the reverse palm down position, lower the body into a suitable dip position, bottom close to the floor but not resting. This can be done one rep per beat, with effort!

6. HAND HELD DUMBBELLS

This exercise can be either alternating biceps curls, lateral raises, running arm action or alternating press above head. Several dumbbell weights can be used to suit all strengths. Only one exercise per circuit session is suitable to create some degree of progression.

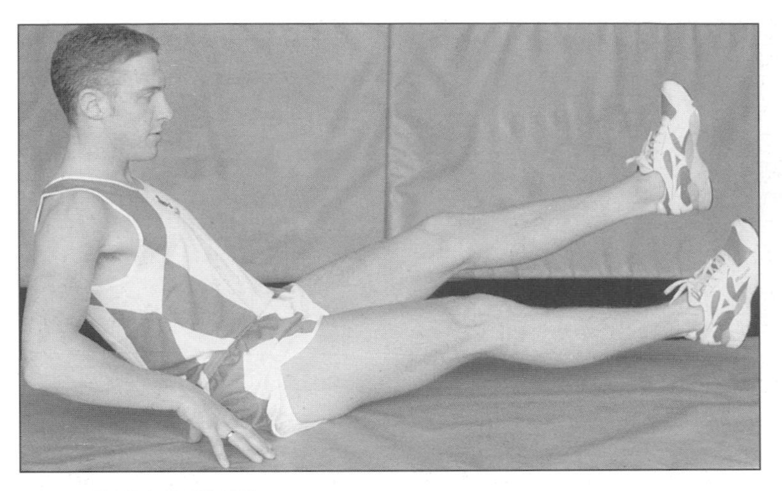

7. LEG WAGGLES

Sit on a mat and extend both legs out in front, lift them a foot off the floor in the extended position and with a slight lean backwards raise the back of the knees off the floor and waggle the legs alternately, keeping them locked. Both hands should be touching the floor at either side with the finger tips. Not an easy exercise with both legs - alternatively do them with single legs in turn.

8. SKI SQUAT POSITION

Initially the position looks easy but it grows on you ! Just sit in a squat position, knees at 90 degrees, legs shoulder width, keep the feet facing straight forward, arms extended out in front. The easier version is with the legs less square, in a more upright position.

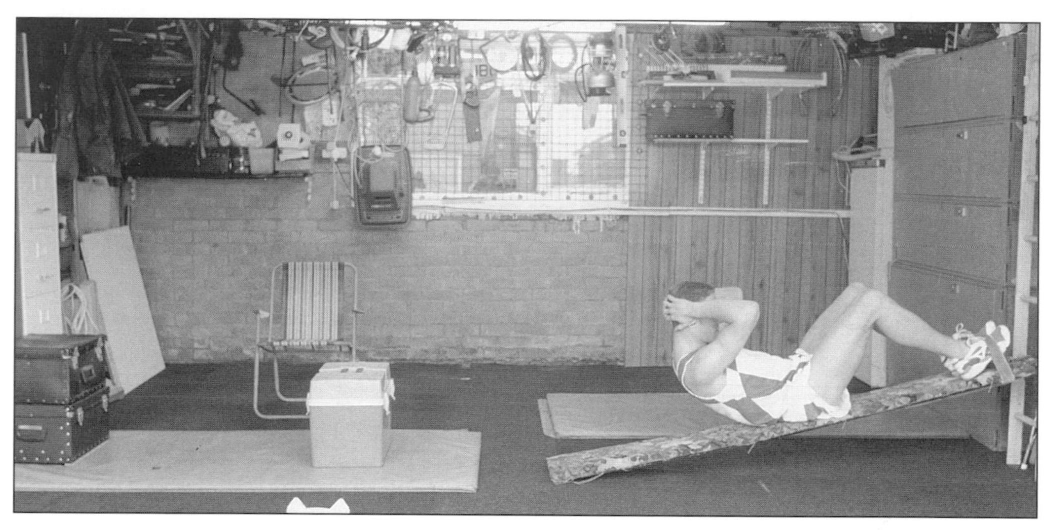

It does not require a well laid out gymnasium to have a succesful circuit.

Depending on the time of the year and the general content of the training schedule, a circuit can be completed once or twice a week. The principle for endurance runners is to create a session that is highly aerobic, with high repetitions and little rest period between stages. Total circuit time of approximately 30 minutes can be judged sufficient in time value. The intensity is variable depending on the condition of the athlete but should enable continuity without pause. The weekly progression is thus by a gradual increase in intensity of effort. The opportunity should not be missed to include a short flexibility routine before the circuit, and a more intense session on completion, when the athlete is thoroughly warmed up.

SUPPLEMENTARY TRAINING ASPECTS

Two extra dimensions in adaptive training can be achieved during a circuit session.

HEAT ADAPTATION

The intensity of a circuit in warm weather conditions can create a degree of overheating that can be considered adaptive training if this aspect is encouraged. Working with covered limbs and suitable clothing can achieve tolerance conditioning. This aspect of physical and mental preparation should not be overlooked.

FLUID INTAKE

For those endurance athletes who by necessity are required to take drink during a race, the circuit session can be utilized for practising this activity. Without stopping, drinks should be taken during the 10 seconds between stages, and total approximately 500 mils for the 30 minutes.

Appendix 3

World Trophy Champions 1985-1995

YEAR VENUE	MENS WINNER SHORT RACE	MENS WINNER LONG RACE
1985 Marebbe. Italy	Kenny Stuart. Eng.	Alfonso Vallicella. Ita.
1986 Morbegno. Italy	M Simonetti. Ita.	Alfonso Vallicella. Ita.
1987 Valbella. Switzerland	Fausto Bonzi. Ita.	Jay Johnson. USA.
1988 Keswick. England	Alfonso Vallicella. Ita.	Dino Tadello. Ita.
1989 Die. France	Fausto Bonzi. Ita.	Jairo Correa. Col.
1990 Telfes. Austria	Severino Bernardini. Ita.	Constantino Bertolla. Ita.
1991 Zermatt. Switzerland	John Lenihan. Ire.	Jairo Correa. Col.
1992 Susa. Italy	Martin Jones. Eng.	Helmut Schmuck. Aut.
1993 Gap. France	Martin Jones. Eng.	
1994 Berchtesgaden. FRG	Helmut Schmuck. Aut.	
1995 Edinburgh. Scotland	L Fergona. Ita.	

YEAR VENUE	LADIES WINNER	JUNIOR WINNER
1985 Marebbe. Italy	Olivia Gruener. FRG.	Gian-Battista Lizzoli. Ita.
1986 Morbegno. Italy	Carol Haigh. Eng.	F Naitza. Ita.
1987 Valbella. Switzerland	Fabiola Rueda. Col.	Fausto Lizzoli. Ita.
1988 Keswick. England	Fabiola Rueda. Col.	Woody Schoch. Switz.
1989 Die. France	Isabelle Guilott. Fra.	Andrea Agostini. Ita.
1990 Telfes. Austria	Beverley Redfern. Sco.	Markus Kroll. Aut.
1991 Zermatt. Switzerland	Isabelle Guilott. Fra.	Ulrich Steidl. FRG.
1992 Susa. Italy	Gudrun Pfluger. Aus.	Maurizio Gemmetto. Ita.
1993 Gap. France	Isabelle Guilott. Fra.	Gabriele De Nard. Ita.
1994 Berchtesgaden. FRG	Gudrun Pfluger. Aus.	Martin Bajcicak. Slovakia.
1995 Edinburgh. Scotland	Gudrun Pfluger. Aus.	M Bonetti. Ita.

Alfonso Vallicella (Italy) Three times winner in a World Trophy event, here competing at Keswick in 1988.

APPENDIX 4

UK Championship Winners

Fell Runner of the Year

MEN

1972	Dave Cannon	Kendal A.C.
1973	Harry Walker	Blackburn Harriers
1974	Jeff Norman	Altrincham A.C.
1975	Mike Short	Horwich RMI Harriers
1976	Martin Weeks	Bingley Harriers
1977	Alan McGee	Keswick A.C.
1978	Mike Short	Horwich RMI Harriers
1979	Andy Styan	Holmfirth Harriers
1980	Billy Bland	Keswick A.C.

British Fell Running Champion

MEN

1981	John Wild	RAF Cosford
1982	John Wild	RAF Cosford
1983	Kenny Stuart	Keswick A.C.
1984	Kenny Stuart	Keswick A.C.
1985	Kenny Stuart	Keswick A.C.
1986	Jack Maitland	Pudsey & Bramley A.C.
1987	Colin Donnelly	Eryri Harriers
1988	Colin Donnelly	Eryri Harriers
1989	Colin Donnelly	Eryri Harriers
1990	Gary Devine	Pudsey & Bramley A.C.
1991	Keith Anderson	Ambleside A.C.
1992	Steve Hawkins	Bingley Harriers
1993	Mark Croasdale	Lancaster & Morecambe A.C.
1994	Mark Kinch	Warrington A.C.
1995	Mark Kinch	Warrington A.C.

British Fell Running Champion

WOMEN

1981	Ros Coates	Lochaber A.C.
1982	Sue Parkin	Airedale & Spen Valley A.C.
1983	Angela Carson	Eryri Harriers
1984	Pauline Howarth	Keswick A.C.
1985	Pauline Howarth	Keswick A.C.
1986	Angela Carson	Eryri Harriers
1987	Jackie Smith	Dark Peak Fell Runners
1988	Clare Crofts	Dark Peak Fell Runners
1989	Ruth Pickvance	Clayton-le Moors Harriers
1990	Trish Calder	Edinburgh Southern Harriers
1991	Trish Calder	Edinburgh Southern Harriers
1992	Clare Crofts	Dark Peak Fell Runners
1993	Angela B Barker	Keswick A.C.
1994	Angela B Barker	Keswick A.C.
1995	Sarah Rowell	Pudsey & Bramley A.C.

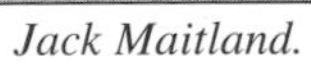

Jack Maitland.

Ruth Pickvance.

Veteran Fell Runner of the Year

1979	Harry Blenkinsop	Kendal A.C.
1980	Ray Aucott	Dark Peak Fell Runners

British Veteran Fell Running Champion

MEN

1981	Tacwyn Davies	Aldershot, Farnham & District A.C.
1982	Ray Aucott	Dark Peak Fell Runners
1983	Paul Murray	Horwich RMI Harriers
1984	Ray Aucott	Dark Peak Fell Runners
1985	Peter Hall	Barrow A.C.
1986	Del Davies	Eryri Harriers
1987	Peter McWade	Clayton-le-Moors Harriers
1988	Billy Bland	Keswick A.C.
1989	Andy Styan	Holmforth Harriers
1990	Dave Spedding	Keswick A.C.
1991	BobWhitfield	Bingley Harriers
1992	BobWhitfield	Bingley Harriers
1993	Mick Hoffe	Ambleside A.C.
1994	Harry Jarret	Cumberland Fell Runners
1995	Steve Jackson	Horwich RMI Harriers

WOMEN

1991	Trish Calder	Edinburgh Southern Harriers
1992	Jackie Smith	Dark Peak Fell Runners
1993	Jackie Smith	Dark Peak Fell Runners
1994	Kath Harvey	Altrincham A.C.
1995	Nicola Davies	Borrowdale Fell Runners

British Super Veteran Fell Running Champion

1983	Peter Carmichael	Morpeth Harriers
1984	Gilbert Scott	Cockermouth A.C.
1985	Bill Gauld	Carnethy Hill Runners
1986	Bill Gauld	Carnethy Hill Runners
1987	Bill Gauld	Carnethy Hill Runners
1988	Danny Hughes	Cumberland Fell Runners
1989	Don Ashton	Blackburn Harriers
1990	Norman Matthews	Horwich RMI Harriers
1991	Roger Bell	Ambleside A.C.
1992	Don Ashton	Blackburn Harriers
1993	John Nuttall	Clayton-le-Moors Harriers
1994	Don Williams	Eryri Harriers
1995	Dave Spedding	Keswick A.C.

Pete McWade.

Roger Bell.

FRA Junior Fell Running Champion

1986	Adrian Jones	Pudsey & Bramley A.C.
1987	Geoff Hall	Holmfirth Harriers
1988	Geoff Hall	Holmfirth Harriers
1989	Gerard Cudahy	Buxton A.C.
1990	William Styan	Holmfirth Harriers
1991	William Styan	Holmfirth Harriers
1992	William Styan	Holmfirth Harriers
1993	Matt Whitfield	Bingley Harriers
1994	Matt Moorhouse	Salford Harriers
1995	Lee Gibson	Cumberland Fell Runners

FRA Intermediate Fell Running Champion

1986	Robin Bergstrand	Rochdale Harriers
1987	Gary Devine	Pudsey & Bramley A.C.
1988	John Taylor	Holmfirth Harriers
1989	John Taylor	Holmfirth Harriers
1990	Gerard Cudahy	Stockport Harriers
1991	Ben Evans	Ambleside A.C.
1992	Patrick Boyd	Blackburn Harriers
1993	Nathan Matthews	Horwich RMI Harriers
1994	Robert Hope	Horwich RMI Harriers
1995	Matthew Wigmore	Helsby R.C.

Geoff Hall.

William Styan.

Nathan Matthews and Patrick Boyd.

English Champions

MEN

1986	Dave Cartridge	Bolton United Harriers
1987	Bob Whitfield	Bingley Harriers
1988	Shaun Livesey	Rossendale Harriers
1989	Gary Devine	Pudsey & Bramley A.C.
1990	Shaun Livesey	Rossendale Harriers
1991	Gavin Bland	Borrowdale Fell Runners
1992	Brian Thompson	Cumberland Fell Runners
1993	Mark Croasdale	Lancaster & Morecambe A.C.
1994	Mark Kinch	Warrington A.C.
1995	Mark Kinch	Warrington A.C.

WOMEN

1986	Carol Haigh	Holmfirth Harriers
1987	Vanessa Brindle	Clayton-le-Woods Harriers
1988	Clare Crofts	Dark Peak FR.
1989	Clare Crofts	Dark Peak FR.
1990	Cheryl Cook	Clayton-le-Moors Harriers
1991	Cheryl Cook	Clayton-le-Moors Harriers
1992	Jackie Smith	Dark Peak Fell Runners
1993	Carol Haigh	Calder Valley Fell Runners
1994	Angela Priestley	Horsforth Fellandale
1995	Sarah Rowell	Pudsey & Bramley A.C.

VETERANS

1986	Dave Cartwright	Penistone Footpath Runners
1987	Peter McWade	Clayton-le-Moors Harriers
1988	Billy Bland	Keswick A.C.
1989	Andy Styan	Holmfirth Harriers
1990	Tony Hesketh	Horwich RMI Harriers
1991	Bob Whitfield	Bingley Harriers
1992	Billy Bland	Borrowdale Fell Runners
1993	Bob Whitfield	Bingley Harriers
1994	Harry Jarrett	Cumberland Fell Runners
1995	Steve Jackson	Horwich RMI Harriers

SUPER VETERANS

1986	George Barras	Skyrac A.C.
1987	Danny Hughes	Cumberland Fell Runners
1988	Danny Hughes	Cumberland Fell Runners
1989	Don Ashton	Blackburn Harriers
1990	Norman Matthews	Horwich RMI Harriers
1991	Roger Bell	Ambleside A.C.
1992	Don Ashton	Blackburn Harriers
1993	Roger Bell	Ambleside A.C.
1994	Bill Toogood	Dark Peak Fell Runners
1995	Dave Spedding	Keswick A.C.

0/60 VETERANS

1993	Dave Hodgson	Horsforth Fellandale
1994	Barry Thackery	Dark Peak Fell Runners
1995	Lawrence Sullivan	Clayton-le-Moors Harriers

WOMEN VETERANS

1991	Trish Calder	Edinburgh Southern
1992	Jackie Smith	Dark Peak Fell Runners
1993	Cecilia Greasley	Macclesfield Harriers
1994	Cecilia Greasley	Macclesfield Harriers
1995	Nicola Davies	Borrowdale Fell Runners

Vanessa (Brindle) Peacock.

Nicola Davies.

Welsh Champions

MEN

1985	Hefin Griffiths	Eryri Harriers
1986	Hefin Griffiths	Eryri Harriers
1987	Hefin Griffiths	Eryri Harriers
1988	Colin Donnelly	Eryri Harriers
1989	Duncan Hughes	Hebog
1990	Duncan Hughes	Hebog
1991	Emlyn Roberts	Eryri Harriers
1992	Steve Hughes	Hebog
1993	Andy Darby	Mynddwyr De Cymru
1994	Simon Forster	Eryri Harriers
1995	Gari Williams	Eryri Harriers

WOMEN

1985	Angela Carson	Eryri Harriers
1986	Angela Carson	Eryri Harriers
1987	Alice Bedwell	Mynddwyr De Cymru
1988	Angela Carson	Eryri Harriers
1989	Stel Farrar	Eryri Harriers
1990	Lydia Kirk	Mynddwyr De Cymru
1991	Jill Teague	Bingley Harriers
1992	Angela B Barker	Keswick A.C.
1993	Angela B Barker	Keswick A.C.
1994	Sharon Woods	Mynddwyr De Cymru
1995	Angela B Barker	Keswick A.C.

Gari Williams

Scottish Champions

MEN

1985	Andy Curtis	Livingston & District A.A.C.
1986	Dermott McGonigle	Dundee University
1987	Andy Curtis	Livingston & District A.A.C.
1988	Alan Farningham	Gala Harriers
1989	Dennis Bell	Haddington East Lothian Pacemakers
1990	David Rodgers	Lochaber A.C
1991	Alan Farningham	Gala Harriers
1992	Andy Kitchin	Livingston & District A.A.C.
1993	David Rodgers	Lochaber A.C.
1994	John Wilkinson	Gala Harriers
1995	Mark Rigby	Westerlands C.C.C.

WOMEN

1985	Ann Curtis	Livingston A.C.
1986	Ann Curtis	Livingston A.C.
1987	C Whalley	Livingston A.C.
1988	Penny Rother	Edinburgh A.C.
1989	Trish Calder	Edinburgh A.C.
1990	Trish Calder	Edinburgh A.C.
1991	Trish Calder	Edinburgh A.C.
1992	Lesley Hope	Lochaber A.C.
1993	Helene Diamantides	Westerlands C.C.C.
1994	Angela B Barker	Eryri Harriers
1995	Christine Menhennet	Westerlands C.C.C.

Dave Rodgers

Northern Ireland Champions

MEN

1986	Ian Parke	Ballydrain Harriers
1987	Jim Patterson	Mourne Fell Runners
1988	Jim Patterson	North Down
1989	Adrian Philpott	Achilles
1990	Adrian Philpott	Achilles
1991	Adrian Philpott	Achilles
1992	Brian Ervine	Ballydrain Harriers
1993	Neil Carty	North Belfast
1994	Brian Ervine	Ballydrain Harriers
1995	Brian Ervine	Ballydrain Harriers

WOMEN

1993	Roma McConville	North Down
1994	Roma McConville	North Down
1995	Roma McConville	North Down

Isle of Man Champions

1985	Tony Varley	Boundry Harriers
1986	Tony Varley	Boundry Harriers
1987	Stephen Hall	Boundry Harriers
1988	Allan Gage	Western A.C.
1989	Tony Varley	Boundry Harriers
1990	Richie Stevenson	Manx Fell Runners
1991	Stephen Hall	Boundry Harriers
1992	Tony Rowley	Manx Fell Runners
1993	Tony Rowley	Manx Fell Runners
1994	Tony Rowley	Manx Fell Runners
1995	Tony Rowley	Manx Fell Runners

Brian Ervine.

Tony Rowley.

Open Fell Running

BAF Rules were amended in 1995 so that an amateur may compete in a non-permitted fell race (that is, not an official FRA Race) without losing amateur status. Members are reminded that only official FRA Races are held under FRA Rules and covered by FRA insurance.

A list of addresses of the various associations can be obtained from the FRA secretary.

Steve Hawkins.

Professional (Open) Champions

NORTHERN SPORTS PROMOTERS ASSOCIATION CHAMPIONSHIP

1970-79	Fred Reeves	Coniston
1980	Kenny Stuart	Threlkeld
1981	Kenny Stuart	Threlkeld
1982	Mick Hawkins	Grassington
1983	Mick Hawkins	Grassington
1984	Mick Hawkins	Grassington

B.O.F.R.A. CHAMPIONSHIP

1985	Steve Carr	Oxenholme	
1986	Steve Carr	Oxenholme	Jointly
	Steve Hawkins	Grassington	
1987	Steve Carr	Oxenholme	
1988	John Atkinson	Ireleth	
1989	John Atkinson	Ireleth	
1990	John Atkinson	Ireleth	
1991	John Atkinson	Ireleth	
1992	Robert Hudson	Malham	
1993	Donald Lee	Salterbeck	
1994	Craig Bottomley	Keighley	
1995	Andy Smith	Skipton